10 Questions to Answer after Serving a Mission

"If your goal is to live a successful life as a disciple of Christ, then this book is perfect for you!"

—Chad Lewis, returned missionary (Taiwan), former NFL player, and author of *Surround Yourself with Greatness*

"A complete must-read for all returned missionaries! This book is a beautiful tool that makes the transition to home life much easier and more effective."

—Tyler Haws, returned missionary (Philippines), BYU basketball's all-time leading scorer

"This book is an all-encompassing guide to the life of a returned missionary. Ben brilliantly addresses myriad challenges (spiritual, physical, marriage, education, career, and so on) that missionaries face when they return home, and he does it in a way that is sure to make you laugh!"

—Hank Smith, returned missionary (California), EFY and Education Week speaker and author

10 QUESTIONS TO ANSWER AFTER SERVING A MISSION

BENJAMIN HYRUM WHITE

CFI
An Imprint of Cedar Fort, Inc.
Springville, Utah

ISBN 13: 978-1-4621-1660-7

Published by CFI, an imprint of Cedar Fort, Inc.
2373 W. 700 S., Springville, UT 84663
Distributed by Cedar Fort, Inc., www.cedarfort.com

LIBRARY OF CONGRESS CATALOGING-IN-PUBLICATION DATA

White, Benjamin Hyrum, 1978- author.
10 questions to answer after serving a mission / Benjamin Hyrum White.
  pages cm
Summary: Ideas to help LDS missionaries to transition after serving a mission.
ISBN 978-1-4621-1660-7 (pbk. : alk. paper)
1. Mormon missionaries--Conduct of life. 2. Mormons--Conduct of life. 3. Adjustment (Psychology)--Religious aspects--Christianity. I. Title. II. Title: Ten questions to answer after serving a mission.

BX8661.W34 2015
266'.9332--dc23

2015014836

Cover design by Shawnda T. Craig
Cover design © 2015 Lyle Mortimer
Edited and typeset by Kevin Haws

Printed in the United States of America

10 9 8 7 6 5 4 3 2 1

Printed on acid-free paper

Contents

Contents

To Keenan Kae,
the single greatest blessing that happened
to me after serving a mission.

Introduction

"It's time to raise the bar not only for missionaries but also for returned missionaries and for your entire generation."[1]

—*Elder M. Russell Ballard*

WELL DONE, MY friend! You have completed one of the great accomplishments of your young life: you honorably served the Lord on a full-time mission for eighteen or twenty-four months. I hope that you came to love the people you so diligently served and, in the process, saw Matthew 16:25 come to pass in your life: "whosoever will lose his life for my sake shall find it." You find out who you really are when you are engaged in the Lord's work.

Because you found yourself while laboring alongside the Savior, returning home can be a big adjustment. I often have a good laugh with my seminary students when I ask them to describe what their older siblings were like when they first returned home from their mission. Many of them make the comment, "He was weird when he came home." They go on to describe some of the

Introduction

missionary zeal that spilled over into their siblings' nametag-less life. Comments such as "He made me read scriptures with him" and "She was always talking about the Church" make me smile. I gently instruct my young friends, saying, "Heaven forbid your brother or sister should want to stay close to the Savior when they come home." I then recount a few of those awkward moments that happened to me after serving a mission.

I know you have experienced them too: listening to the radio again, being alone, wearing "normal clothes" all the time, and readjusting to electronics. But the blueprints for success as a missionary on the mission are not too different than the blueprints for success when you return home.

With any luck, you are now practicing what you preached on your mission. Think of how often you invited people to have faith in Christ and His Atonement, repent, be baptized, receive the gift of the Holy Ghost, and endure to the end. This was part of your mission every day! Now you get to put this formula called discipleship into practice for the rest of your life. Paul explained to the Corinthians, "Even so hath the Lord ordained that they which preach the gospel should live of the gospel" (1 Corinthians 9:14). Instead of *Preach My Gospel*, now it is time to *Live My Gospel*! Jesus expressed it in these words: "If any man will come after me, let him deny himself, and take up his cross, and follow me" (Matthew 16:24).

Walking after the Lord is not for the faint of heart. You know from your mission experiences as well as I do that if you want to follow Christ, He will take you hiking. Look at what the Savior did just before giving arguably His greatest sermon. After seeing

Introduction

the Savior teaching, preaching, and healing, multitudes gathered to be around Him. The Gospel of Matthew reads, "And seeing the multitudes, he went up into a mountain" (Matthew 5:1).

This might be a stretch, but I can see the great Creator testing the massive throng of people to see who would be willing to make the arduous journey to the top of the mountain. Matthew continued, "And when he was set, his disciples came unto him" (ibid.). Notice that only disciples followed Him to the top. I wonder if many in the multitude were fascinated by a man who could work miracles and came out of curiosity to see Him. I wonder if many did not make the journey up the mountain because they thought, *Surely He has to come down sometime. I'm too tired to hike all that way.* Others might have complained that they did not have the right shoes. In any case, after the novelty or excitement of seeing Jesus do great works, the realities of a long, possibly mundane hike up a mountain set in. Only those with knees willing to bend and lungs willing to breathe heavily will truly reap the reward of the Bread of Life because, upon arriving at the top, Jesus gave them some of the greatest food ever served to the soul.

One of the factors that brought about the creation of *Preach My Gospel* was President Gordon B. Hinckley's concern about convert retention. He said, "There is absolutely no point in doing missionary work unless we hold on to the fruits of that effort."[2] A lesser-known impetus behind *Preach My Gospel* was another of President Hinckley's concerns about missionary work: the lack of returned missionary retention. Elder Jeffrey R. Holland remembered a conversation he had with the prophet about this subject when he said, "That was the thing that was bothering President

Introduction

Hinckley. . . . Why can a missionary come home and be inactive? [President Hinckley] said, 'I don't understand that. There are a lot of things in life I understand, but I don't understand that. How can a missionary come home and go inactive?'"[3] In the same meeting, Elder Holland went on to teach that *Preach My Gospel* "is supposed to get in your bones, it is supposed to be down in the marrow of your soul. The most important contact and conversion, investigator and baptism you will ever have is yourself. In a way we could say that your mission will be a success if you don't convert anybody but yourself. It will still be worth it and it will still be right and it will still have its impact."[4]

This is why I am writing to you. My hope is that you will continue to be faithful now that you have served an honorable full-time mission. I hope your conversion to the Savior and His restored gospel will remain as you "lay aside every . . . sin which doth so easily beset [you], and let us run with patience the race that is set before us, looking unto Jesus the author and finisher of our faith" (Hebrews 12:1–2). That way, you can stand with confidence in the presence of God one day and say, "I have fought a good fight, I have finished my course, I have kept the faith: Henceforth there is laid up for me a crown of righteousness, which the Lord, the righteous judge, shall give me at that day" (2 Timothy 4:7–8).

Your full-time service as a missionary is now over, but your full-time jump into adulthood is just beginning! I hope the following ten questions will give you an opportunity to ponder and prepare for a faithful life of discipleship. May I suggest you read a chapter a day and look for ways to implement some of

Introduction

the promptings of the Spirit, which will teach you how to "press forward with a steadfastness in Christ" (2 Nephi 31:20) now that you are home? The ten questions are specifically designed to be open-ended, necessitating a thoughtful answer instead of a simple yes or no response. You can even take notes in the book as needed. There are also additional readings at the end of every chapter so you can dive more fully into each subject with words from the scriptures, living prophets, and those I feel have given profound counsel on each topic.

Elder Ballard's talk in the October 2002 general conference effectively "raised the bar" for missionary preparation. This call for "the greatest generation of missionaries" spurred the writing of my first book: *10 Questions to Answer While Preparing for a Mission*. Now he has reissued this call to raise the bar, but for the greatest generation of young adults in the Church. You now fit into this category. Go back and reread this talk from the April 2015 general conference. Elder Ballard asked some pointed questions, akin to Alma 5, that will give you a chance for some personal introspection. This is my favorite piece of counsel he gave:

> I remind you returned missionaries that your preparation for life and for a family should be continuous. 'RM' doesn't mean 'retired Mormon'! . . . Please use the skills you learned on your mission to bless the lives of people around you every day. Do not shift your focus from serving others to focusing exclusively on school, work, or social activities. Instead, balance your life with spiritual experiences that remind and prepare you for continued, daily ministering to others.[5]

Introduction

Again, congratulations on finishing your mission journey and welcome to the high adventure of hiking after the Master!

Additional Reading

- M. Russell Ballard, "The Greatest Generation of Young Adults," *Ensign*, May 2015

Notes

1. M. Russell Ballard, "The Greatest Generation of Young Adults," *Ensign*, May 2015.
2. Gordon B. Hinckley, "Find the Lambs, Feed the Sheep," *Ensign*, May 1999.
3. Jeffrey R. Holland, January 13, 2009 Missionary Training Center Devotional. See author's Master's thesis entitled "The History of *Preach My Gospel*," in the *Religious Educator* 14, no. 1 (2013): 129–58. Available at rsc.byu.edu.
4. Ibid.
5. M. Russell Ballard, "The Greatest Generation of Young Adults," *Ensign*, May 2015.

Question 1

How Will I Adjust from *Preach My Gospel* to *Live My Gospel*?

"The adjustment associated with leaving the mission field and returning to the world you left behind is sometimes difficult."[1]

—*Elder L. Tom Perry*

ONE OF THE first adjustments I had to make upon returning home from my mission in Colorado was interacting with women again. Sure, you talk with the opposite gender all the time as a missionary, but now the nature of your relationship to them has changed. You are no longer limited to just a handshake. My brother Rick was quick to help me make this transition. He told me that there was a young single adult dance on Friday—two days after I got home. I agreed to go even though I was scared to death. It is quite ironic that I had no problem walking up to a stranger's house and, after a brief introduction, spilling my guts with them about God and the mysteries of the universe, and now all I needed to do was have similar conversations while rotating in clockwise circles with a hand on a random woman's hip. No problem, right? Yikes!

10 Questions to Answer
after Serving a Mission

I am sure that you understand exactly what I am talking about, even if you turned counterclockwise during those first conversations home from your mission. Needless to say, nothing much happened for me with the female folk on this occasion. I heard a lot of new music and I was so intimidated that I only danced with girls I knew before my mission. But it was a good step in the right direction of reintegrating back into normal, post-mission life.

This is one example of the many adjustments you are or will continue to make upon returning home from missionary service. The example I gave is a bit trivial compared to some of the bigger questions you might have upon returning home, like where and when should I go to school? What should my major be? Should I get a job? How do I balance school with all the other activities I have going on? Is he (or she) "the one"? These and many other questions are real and can make you feel like a deer in the headlights, with so much uncertainty ahead of you.

Think of it this way. Up to this point in your young life, much of it has been planned for you, or there have been significant milestones to mark the path. At eight years old, you get baptized. At twelve, you enter the young men's or women's program as a deacon or Beehive. At fourteen, you transition to the teacher's quorum or Mia Maid group and can attend stake dances. At sixteen, you can date and drive, and you become a Laurel or a priest, who now has the power to baptize and bless the sacrament. And at eighteen, you are a legal adult, and high school graduation is here. For many, this also means mission time—which includes the honor of holding the Melchizedek Priesthood for the men—and going to the temple to receive your endowment. Once your mission is completed, you still have long-term goals like school and being sealed in the temple to your eternal companion, but now there is no set timetable for how to get there, or when.

I want you to understand an important principle that will help with your newfound uncertainty for this wonderful time in your life. Early in the history of the Church, Joseph Smith would frequently have family and friends petition him to receive a revelation from the Lord on their behalfs. The early sections of the Doctrine and Covenants showed Joseph's prophetic abilities in receiving answers for various individuals wanting to know how they could assist in the Lord's work. As the newly established Church grew, revelation and persecution drove them to Kirtland Ohio in 1831. As the will of the Lord continued to unfold, more and more members of the Church wanted to know their duty in relation to how they could assist the cause of establishing Zion. With a growing population in the Church, I imagine it would simply be impossible for Joseph Smith to continue receiving revelation for individuals day after day. There were so many other things for the Prophet to attend to. It is within this broader context that Doctrine and Covenants 58:26–29 was given:

> For behold, it is not meet that I should command in all things; for he that is compelled in all things, the same is a slothful and not a wise servant; wherefore he receiveth no reward.
>
> Verily I say, men should be anxiously engaged in a good cause, and do many things of their own free will, and bring to pass much righteousness;

For the power is in them, wherein they are agents unto themselves. And inasmuch as men do good they shall in nowise lose their reward.

But he that doeth not anything until he is commanded, and receiveth a commandment with doubtful heart, and keepeth it with slothfulness, the same is damned.

Now, "anxiously engaged" does not mean that you are a jittery fiancé (though you might feel that way sometime later in life). What it does mean is that you are *eagerly involved* in good causes along the path your life is taking. Just as Joseph Smith could not tell each member of the Church what they individually needed to do, you should not expect everyone else to tell you where to go to school, what to major in, and whom to marry. The Lord can help you with these mammoth undertakings, but use your God-given agency "to act . . . and not be acted upon" (2 Nephi 2:26). Use your free will to make righteous choices instead of just reacting to the choices others have made.

A companion lesson to the power to act comes shortly after D&C 58. I imagine the Lord teaching the Saints that they do not need to be commanded in every little thing when He said: "It mattereth not to me." The Lord repeats this principle four times[2] in D&C 60–63. In each of these scriptural injunctions, there was something that mattered to God and something that did not. Generally speaking, what mattered to the Lord was that the elders traveled speedily to their destinations while bearing testimony and helping the Saints gather. What did not matter to the Lord was whether they should travel on land or on water, whether they should make a craft or buy one, or whether the elders journeyed all together or two by two.

How Will I Adjust from *Preach My Gospel* to *Live My Gospel*?

As you blaze your own trail in life, you will find the Lord is concerned about where you are going but allows you the chance to determine how you are going to get there. While some of the details matter not to God, rest assured that *you* matter to Him. He wants to help you along the path, but I think He frequently will allow you the full gift of your power to act in order to see just how you will do it.

Therefore, do not get discouraged if you petition for His help and you do not get immediate or powerful promptings about what to do. In the mission field, you surely experienced His divine direction of where to go, what to do, and what to say. Continue to apply these words: "Trust in the Lord with all thine heart; and lean not unto thine own understanding. In all thy ways acknowledge him, and he shall direct thy paths" (Proverbs 3:5–6), even if you feel unsure of what path to take. Elder Christofferson said, "Take responsibility and go to work so that there is something for God to help us with."[3]

Brother Matthew Holland, the president of Utah Valley University, told an insightful story about taking wrong roads that might actually give you some reassurance. As a seven-year-old boy, he took a trip with his father, Elder Jeffrey R. Holland, in order to experience the sweeping vista of one of the world's beautiful wonders, the Grand Canyon. After enjoying the wondreous scenery and with the sun setting, father and son headed home but had only gone a few miles when they stopped with uncertainty at a fork in the road. With the impending darkness closing in, choosing the right path was imperative. After turning to the Lord in prayer, Elder Holland asked his young son which direction they should go. Matthew felt they should go left, to which his father agreed.

After traveling for only ten minutes down this road, it abruptly dead-ended. They doubled back, this time taking the correct path to the right and still had enough light to travel home. Matthew was troubled. He asked his father, "Why did we both feel like Heavenly Father told us to go down the road to the left when it was the wrong road?" Elder Holland confirmed that he had been given the same impression to go left. He then instructed his young son:

> "The Lord has taught us an important lesson today. Because we were prompted to take the road to the left, we quickly discovered which one was the right one. When we turned around and got on the right road, I was able to travel along its many unfamiliar twists and turnoffs perfectly confident I was headed in the right direction. If we had started on the right road, we might have driven for 30 minutes or so, become uneasy with the unfamiliar surroundings, and been tempted to turn back. If we had done that, we would have discovered the dead-end so late that it would have been too dark to find our way back in totally unfamiliar territory."

Brother Holland has counted this as an unforgettable lesson in his life. He summed up this lesson at the end of the article.

> Sometimes in response to prayers, the Lord may guide us down what *seems* to be the wrong road—or at least a road we don't understand—so, in due time, He can get us firmly and without question on the right road. Of course, He would never lead us down a path of sin, but He might lead us

down a road of valuable experience. Sometimes in our journey through life we can get from point A to point C only by taking a short side road to point B. We had prayed that we could make it safely home that day, and we did.[4]

I think this story serves as a fantastic example of how the next few years of your life might unfold. In the process of being anxiously engaged, you will find yourself exploring uncharted territory. Do not be discouraged if along the way you encounter some dead ends. The Lord not only opens doors for us, but He also will close other doors along the way. Trust Him, and "let us learn to say not only, 'Thy will be done,' but patiently also, 'Thy timing be done.'"[5]

Elder Richard G. Scott gave a remarkable talk about prayer a few years ago in general conference that will be a tremendous aid for you in getting essential answers from God as to the direction of your life. Please read it. In one portion of the talk, he discussed how we can either get a yes or no answer from the Lord, referencing D&C 9:8–9. Then he approached a situation with prayer we have all faced. What do we do when we don't get an answer? His response to this is helpful.

> What do you do when you have prepared carefully, have prayed fervently, waited a reasonable time for a response, and still do not feel an answer? You may want to express thanks when that occurs, for it is an evidence of His trust. When you are living worthily and your choice is consistent with the Savior's teachings and you need to act, proceed with trust. As you are sensitive to the promptings of the Spirit, one of two things will certainly occur at the appropriate

time: either the stupor of thought will come, indicating an improper choice, or the peace or the burning in the bosom will be felt, confirming that your choice was correct. When you are living righteously and are acting with trust, God will not let you proceed too far without a warning impression if you have made the wrong decision.[6]

As you continue to pursue a path for your life that is pleasing to both you and the Lord, let me offer a piece of counsel that answers the question, "What now?" My response to this question is to continue using *Preach My Gospel* as your guide. Apply the contents of this inspired book to your life as a returned missionary. For example, I am sure you memorized and frequently recited your purpose as a missionary. Let me provide a new purpose for you as a returned missionary. Take notice of the contrast.

Your purpose as a missionary is to: "Invite **others** to come unto Christ by **helping them receive** the restored gospel through faith in Jesus Christ and His Atonement, repentance, **baptism**, **receiving** the gift of the Holy Ghost, and enduring to the end."	Your purpose as a **returned** missionary is to: "Invite **yourself** to come unto Christ by **living** the restored gospel through faith in Jesus Christ and His Atonement, repentance, **partaking of the sacrament**, **following** the gift of the Holy Ghost, and enduring to the end."

How Will I Adjust from *Preach My Gospel* to *Live My Gospel*?

The transition from taking care of everyone else to worrying about yourself can be a difficult one. Whereas you were only concerned with helping others come unto Christ for eighteen or twenty-four months, now you have to practice what you preached. You have to live what you so vigorously taught those around you as a missionary.

Do not look at this next stage in your life as being selfish, as much as it is an opportunity to prepare yourself for lifelong service in the kingdom of God.

Look at each of the chapters in *Preach My Gospel* and how they can apply to your life right now. Each one of them can be slightly modified to help you adjust to your life as a returned missionary.

- Chapter 1: What is my purpose as a returned missionary?
- Chapter 2: How do I study effectively now that I am home and for the rest of my life?
- Chapter 3: How do I live and apply what I've taught?
- Chapter 4: Am I still recognizing the Spirit in my life?
- Chapter 5: What role does the Book of Mormon play in my life now?
- Chapter 6: Am I still developing Christlike attributes?
- Chapter 7: How am I going to continue using my mission language? (If applicable.)
- Chapter 8: Am I still setting and keeping goals and using my time wisely?
- Chapter 9: Am I still finding people to share the gospel with— and finding someone to marry? ☺

10 Questions to Answer after Serving a Mission

- Chapter 10: Am I keeping my teaching skills sharp by magnifying my calling?
- Chapter 11: Am I keeping my covenants with the Savior?
- Chapter 12: How will I prepare for my next temple ordinance?
- Chapter 13: How will I work well with my new stake and ward leaders?

So instead of discarding your *Preach My Gospel* manual now that you are home from the mission field, use it as a springboard into the new challenges of your young life. Just as "the Lord of the vineyard labored also with" (Jacob 5:72) you in the mission field, He will not leave you now that you have come home. The challenges and scenery in the vineyard may have changed, but the Savior will still work with you as you seek His help in the new furrows of your life.

A seemingly trivial adjustment all returned missionaries have to make is returning to the land of normal fashion again. With your wardrobe options having been rather narrow for many months, your newfound choices for your appearance are endlessly before you. Though you might feel like swinging the pendulum far away from missionary life, I would caution you to exercise some restraint. I will not present a list of specific dos and don'ts when it comes to fashion (because everyone knows I don't have any anyway). Instead, I will appeal to the Brethren and allow you to apply the Holy Ghost to decide for yourself what matters and what "mattereth not" to the Lord. In speaking to returned missionaries, Elder M. Russell Ballard taught, "We expect you to always look and act like one of His disciples.

Look the part. Act the part. Don't follow worldly trends and fashions. You are better than that."[7] Two other Apostles have echoed this sentiment.[8]

In addition to *Preach My Gospel*, another valuable text all returned missionaries can use is Alma 38. Here we have a wise father talking to his stalwart returned missionary son after they served a mission to the apostate Zoramites. Pour over the contents of this scripture chapter, and I honestly believe that the Holy Ghost can teach you profound insights about your adjustment to returned missionary life. I will share one insight from this chapter now and another one in chapter eight of this book.

Alma teaches Shiblon not to "pray to be heard of men, and to be praised for their wisdom. Do not say: O God, I thank thee that we are better than our brethren" (Alma 38:13–14). With all your newfound skills and attributes you gained in the mission field, do not let it go to your head. "See that ye are not lifted up unto pride; yea, see that ye do not boast in your own wisdom, nor of your much strength" (Alma 38:11).

I have seen some returned missionaries come home from the mission field with an invincibility complex. They are not afraid to flex their newfound spiritual and intellectual muscles to prove how well they know their scriptures in an effort to smack down any whom they perceive as inferior. Still be humble after your mission. Do not be a know-it-all, especially among your family members.

Let me be honest with you—I have had the honor of teaching the scriptures for many years now as a full-time religious educator. The more I learn, the more I realize I do not know all that much. My eyes continue to be opened to the beauties of the Savior's gospel and the power of His grace. My favorite example of true piety and humility is the lesser-known parable of the publican in Luke 18:9–14.

> And he spake this parable unto certain which trusted in themselves that they were righteous, and despised others:
>
> Two men went up into the temple to pray; the one a Pharisee, and the other a publican.
>
> The Pharisee stood and prayed thus with himself, God, I thank thee, that I am not as other men are, extortioners, unjust, adulterers, or even as this publican.
>
> I fast twice in the week, I give tithes of all that I possess.
>
> And the publican, standing afar off, would not lift up so much as his eyes unto heaven, but smote upon his breast, saying, God be merciful to me a sinner.
>
> I tell you, this man went down to his house justified rather than the other: for every one that exalteth himself shall be abased; and he that humbleth himself shall be exalted.

The scene I imagine from verse 13 stirs my heart. I have known many of these simple, salt-of-the-earth servants of the Lord, whose only real desire is to be found clean from sin. That is the greatest desire of my own heart. I want to be clean when I stand before God again. Part of your adjustment to post-mission life will be allowing the beauty of your newfound walk with Christ to shine through your eyes, countenance, and example.

Alma 39–42 are also great chapters for retuned missionary. Whereas Shiblon served faithfully, his younger brother Corianton made some serious mistakes. For any of my early returned missionaries, there is a great lesson to be learned from Corianton, who initially failed his father on his mission to the Zoramites. Later in Corianton's life, we have a brief reference in Alma 48:17–19 about how great Captain Moroni and the sons of Mosiah were. Notice it also includes the sons of Alma. This leads me to believe that Corianton made the necessary changes to continue preaching the word of God.[9] At least a year later, he was among those who continued preaching in Alma 49:30. As further proof of his change of heart, Mormon spoke highly of Shiblon in Alma 63:1–2 and included Corianton in that compliment. Alma 63:10–11 says that Shiblon would have conferred the sacred record on Corianton if he had been home, instead of helping the people who sailed north. It sounds to me like there was enough trust in Corianton's full repentance and faithful conversion after his mistakes.

Chad Lewis, a returned missionary and a former BYU and NFL tight end, wrote a book that might be of help in your adjustment to returning from your mission. It is entitled *Surround Yourself with Greatness*. I recommend that you read it because it teaches some valuable life lessons. One of them I have seen clearly manifested in my own life. Who you consistently surround yourself with in life will have a tremendous influence on what you think, how you speak, and what path you will travel. Now that you have arrived home, do not turn back to old habits or poor friends from before your mission. Do not surrender the high ground you achieved in following the Master! Elder Robert D. Hales taught, "There's a marvelous lesson to be taught by those who live in the islands. When they catch crabs, they place them in a small, flat basket. If you place one crab in the basket, it crawls right out. If you place two crabs in the basket, every time one crab starts to crawl out, it is pulled back in by the other crab. Does that tell you something about your friends?"[10]

The friends I made in high school had a significant impact on the trajectory of my life. I learned to love the Savior, His Church, and the seminary program. Upon returning from my mission, I continued to interact with my now returned missionary friends from my teenage years and made new friends in my Church wards, school classes, and clubs on campus. They helped me eagerly follow the path of returned missionary discipleship. I still hold many of them in my own personal hall of fame for their willingness to walk after the Master. Be wise in who you consistently surround yourself with now that you are home. I hope your family can and will be a safe harbor to return to from time to time. But now is your chance to move forward on your own voyage in life, so make your crew selections with prayerful precision. "The friends you choose will either help or hinder your success."[11]

Above all, with your return to "civilian life," please remember that your missionary work is not done. I have heard some returned missionaries erroneously think that because they have "put in their time," their missions are over. Not a chance! If you truly "became a missionary"[12] before and during your mission, then you realize that sharing the gospel is a lifelong calling. Elder David A. Bednar has apostolically invited us, as members of the Church, "to sweep the earth as with a flood" by "communicating gospel messages through social media."[13] Please continue using technology to spread the message of the gospel. Keep in touch with your former investigators and friends you made in the mission field. I must confess, I have been poor at doing this since returning from my mission—but you have the advantages of modern technology. Help from a distance those whom you so powerfully helped in person.

Elder Neil L. Andersen said it best:

> If you're not a full-time missionary with a missionary badge pinned on your coat, now is the time to paint one on your heart—painted, as Paul said, "not with ink, but with the Spirit of the living God." And returned missionaries, find your old missionary tag. Don't wear it, but put it where you can see it. The Lord needs you now more than ever to be an instrument in His hands. All of us have a contribution to make to this miracle.[14]

As you successfully adjust to the new demands of returned missionary life, the joy of sharing the gospel should still be an integral part of who you are as a disciple of Christ.

Additional Readings

- Alma 37–42
- *Preach My Gospel*
- Richard G. Scott, "Using the Supernal Gift of Prayer," *Ensign*, May 2007
- L. Tom Perry, "The Returned Missionary," *Ensign*, October 2001
- Chad Lewis, *Surround Yourself with Greatness*

10 Questions to Answer after Serving a Mission

Notes

1. L. Tom Perry, "The Returned Missionary," *Ensign*, November 2001.

2. D&C 60:5; 61:22; 62:5; 63:40.

3. D. Todd Christofferson, "Free Forever, to Act for Themselves," *Ensign*, November 2014.

4. Matthew Holland, "Wrong Roads and Revelation," *New Era*, July 2005. (This has been made into a "Mormon Message," with Elder Jeffrey R. Holland narrating.)

5. Neal A. Maxwell, "Plow in Hope," *Ensign*, May 2001.

6. Richard G. Scott, "Using the Supernal Gift of Prayer," *Ensign*, May 2007.

7. M. Russell Ballard, "The Greatest Generation of Missionaries," *Ensign*, November 2002.

8. "I call on you returned missionaries to rededicate yourselves, to become reinfused with the desire and spirit of missionary service. I call on you to look the part, to be the part, and to act the part of a servant of our Father in Heaven." (L. Tom Perry, "The Returned Missionary," *Ensign*, November 2001.)

"Our young elders are models of young manhood. When they come home, some are criticized as being self-righteous for maintaining a decent appearance and keeping their hair trimmed neatly. I cannot understand why a returned missionary is considered self-righteous if he tries to live the standards and principles he has taught as a representative of the Lord to the people where he has served.

Of course returned missionaries are not expected to wear white shirts and ties all of the time. But wearing sloppy clothes and weird hairstyles to supposedly look trendy is not proper for one who holds the divine commission of the priesthood. Returned missionaries are an example to the young men of the Aaronic Priesthood, who will be the future missionaries. Often that which is *seen* by the Aaronic Priesthood is more powerful and persuasive than what is *said*." (James E. Faust, "The Power of Self-Mastery," *Ensign*, May 2000.)

9. Thanks to my friend Rob Elzey for sharing this insight with me.

10. Robert D. Hales, "This Is the Way; and There Is None Other Way," BYU Devotional, January 10, 1982.

11. Thomas S. Monson, "In Harm's Way," *Ensign*, May 1998.

12. David A. Bednar, "Becoming a Missionary," *Ensign*, November 2005.

13. David A. Bednar, "To Sweep the Earth As with a Flood," BYU Education Week, August 19, 2014.

14. Neil L. Andersen, "It's a Miracle," *Ensign*, May 2013.

Question 2

How Can I Perform My Physical and Spiritual Calisthenics Daily?

"Please keep alive the practice of regular individual and companion scripture study. . . . Maybe it is time that we rekindle our missionary spirit through more frequent, consistent, and mighty prayer."[1]

—*Elder L. Tom Perry*

ONE OF MY high school gym coaches used to always "preach" to us about the benefits of physical exercise. More than any other P.E. teacher I ever had, Coach Kemper was sold on the profits of moving your body. He would especially talk about the benefits of running. After taking our warm-up lap around the track, Coach Kemper would seize the opportunity to teach us as we stopped to catch our breath. One of his teachings that has stuck with me over the years was what he called "Zoogies." Zoogies are the cells in our bodies that are lazy. The reason we needed to exercise, he would say, is to get the capillaries in our cells opened from end to end, causing our bodies to move blood at a higher level. Our bodies were then required to build better cells to handle the increased physical movement. As the new, more efficient cells were built, the old Zoogies were jettisoned from our bodies.

I know this is an immense oversimplification of an incredibly complex dynamic within the body, but as a fifteen-year-old young man, I understood what my coach was trying to teach me. The more you train your body to expect moderate to maximum physical exercise on a consistent basis, the more your body will respond with an increased capacity to live up to that expectation.

Exercising consistently is one of the commitments in *Preach My Gospel*. The missionary daily schedule was altered to give missionaries a half hour of exercise every day as part of their morning routine. When I was a missionary, if we wanted any physical activity in the morning, we just had to get up earlier. With sleep at a premium for me in the mission field, exercise did not happen often. Whether you took the exercise time seriously or not on your mission, I would invite you to do so now.

Taking care of your body will bring tremendously positive results not only now but in the long term. I would call the physical activity you should engage in daily calisthenics. Calisthenics consist "of a variety of exercises . . . generally without using equipment or apparatus. They are intended to increase body strength and flexibility . . . using only one's body weight for resistance. . . . When performed vigorously and with variety, calisthenics can benefit both muscular and cardiovascular fitness, in addition to improving . . . balance, agility, and coordination."[2] These kind of exercises could include push-ups, sit-ups, pull-ups, lunges, and jumping jacks.

10 Questions to Answer
after Serving a Mission

For simplicity's sake, I will refer to calisthenics as "the basics." These are the kinds of physical exercises you can do anywhere, without assistance of a gym membership. All the health benefits of engaging in these types of physical activity are well documented and can be found in a multitude of scientific places. I will not outline here a specific regimen for your personal workouts, but I will show you the direct connections between your physical activity and the spiritual sensitivity it can bring to your life.

In addition to physical exercise, eating right will have a huge influence on your body as well as your spirit. The topic of eating right can be highly subjective, not to mention quite sensitive for many people. This is such a hot-button issue that eating fads of one kind or another crop up all the time, extoling their virtues of weight loss or better health. Do not be fooled by such pop culture nonsense. Real nutrition is not found in the extremes. True commitment to eating right does not mean swallowing a magic pill that will allow you to indulge in gluttony and physical apathy. A true commitment to physical health will include appropriate physical activity and disciplined eating consumption.

The most divine guidance we have in this dispensation is found in Doctrine and Covenants 89. Please take the whole section as your guide. We have such a culture as Latter-day Saints to pontificate the virtues of *not* smoking or drinking alcohol, coffee, or tea that we forget the larger portion of this revelation, the parts that tell us what *to do*. Sure, abstaining from these harmful substances can prolong your life, but will the quality of that life be better?

How Can I Perform My Physical and Spiritual Calisthenics Daily?

Real nutrition and commitment to eating the kinds of food the Lord outlines in the Word of Wisdom will be an unfathomable benefit. We focus so much on not forming addictions to drugs and the other don'ts of this revelation without realizing many of the food addictions we already have become slave to. Read Doctrine and Covenants 89 with a prayer of humility. You will find divine assistance as you seek to better nourish this incredible instrument—your body—that the Lord has given you.

Of course, the Word of Wisdom has many more spiritual benefits than it does physical. Once you have committed to take care of your mind and heart physically, revelation can flow more easily. Look at D&C 8:2–3: "I will tell you in your mind and in your heart, by the Holy Ghost, which shall come upon you and which shall dwell in your heart. Now, behold, this is the spirit of revelation." Elder Richard G. Scott said,

> Spiritual communication can be enhanced by good health practices. Exercise, reasonable amounts of sleep, and good eating habits increase our capacity to receive and understand revelation. We will live for our appointed life span. However, we can improve both the quality of our service and our well-being by making careful, appropriate choices. It is important that our daily activities do not distract us from listening to the Spirit.[3]

When speaking about the purpose of the plan of salvation, we quickly rattle off the need to have a physical body. Elder David A. Bednar gave a masterful talk that explores more deeply why we need a physical body. Please study it. In one portion, he briefly addressed the need to have adequate sleep and gives a timely application as to why. "It is impossible for the Spirit to shine in and through our physical bodies when we are dozy and dull from foolishly going to bed at 1:30 a.m. or 2:30 a.m. or later night after night after night (see D&C 88:124)."[4]

A warning about being too hyper-focused on the physical. While it is important to take care of your God-given body, if you become excessive with the physical, you can find your spiritual alignment out of whack. Focus can become fanaticism if not measured with moderation. Observation can become obsession if it is not wielded with wisdom. Be careful with your commitments to physical activity and appetite, and be judicious with the time and effort you put into the physical so it does not cross the line into behavior that take away from you or your loved ones. Balance is a key word in more ways than one when it comes to taking care of the divine body God has given you.

If physical calisthenics are the basics for physical exercise, then what would you consider to be spiritual calisthenics? The basics are daily prayer and scripture study. You know the difference between saying your prayers and talking to God. Additionally, you know the difference between reading your scriptures and studying the Word of God. If your commitment to these fundamental basic building blocks of diligent discipleship has wavered, I invite you to reinvest in your covenant—not just your commitment—to God. Elder Bednar described this when talking about partaking of the sacrament:

> I want to draw your attention to the second covenantal obligation to "always remember him." I do not know of a better way to always remember him than to daily study the

scriptures. That covenant is not an abstract notion. It can be honored in meaningful, personal prayer every morning and night and in diligent study of the scriptures.

When I served as a stake president and interviewed literally hundreds of members of the Church, I frequently would ask, "Do you remember and keep the covenants you have made?" I do not recall many people answering no. When I would inquire further and ask about their scripture study, some would say, "I do not have time." Then I would ask about their personal prayers, and the answer often was, "I am not as consistent as I should be." On some occasions I would then inquire, "Do you, in fact, keep the covenant to always remember Him?"

The covenants we make in the waters of baptism are a commitment to always remember him, in part through meaningful prayer and diligent study of the scriptures.[5]

I love talking to my Father in Heaven. I know He hears me and will answer my prayers in His time. This was the first testimony that I "learned for myself" (Joseph Smith—History 1:20). I also know you have a testimony of the power of prayer. I am positive you have sacred experiences from your mission where the Lord answered your prayers frequently, and maybe even immediately. Do not give up now that you are home. Have patience if some of your prayers right now seem unanswered. Think of how long Alma the Elder and his wife surely prayed for divine intercession with their wayward son. They did not falter in their divine petitions, and neither should you.

I once heard a former stake president of mine say, "Our relationship to the words of Christ will determine our relationship with Christ." I also heard a high councilman state this beautiful truth: "When I learned to give the Lord my precious time and not just my spare time is when the scriptures came alive for me." If you are drinking deeply from the reservoir of living water, please continue to do so. If you are not enjoying such spiritual refreshment, it is time to quench your thirst.

My good friend Boubacar Barry taught me a profound lesson while we were part of the International Folk Dance Ensemble at BYU. Out of the blue, he approached me one day in class, put a hand on my shoulder, and said, "Feed me." Without any food to provide him, I responded, "Sorry, Boubacar, I don't have any food." Not one to be dissuaded, he repeated, "Feed me." With a bit of exasperation, I replied, "I still don't have any food." I said I could go get something from the vending machine if he was really that hungry. With a twinkle in his eye, Boubacar shook his head. "No, no, no, Ben," and, with emphasis, said, "Feed me!"

I felt as sharp as a marble at this point because I realized he was referring to spiritual food. "Oh!" I said as a smile crept across my face to match his. I thought for a moment about what I taught as a student teacher in my seminary class that morning. As I was about to give Boubacar the gospel goodness, he abruptly stuck his hand in my face and said, "Nope. You blew it," and he walked away. I felt indignant. "Come back here!" I wanted to shout, but I just shook my head and smiled as my friend left.

About a week later, Boubacar surprised me again with a hand on my shoulder as he politely requested, "Feed me." I am so slow that I first thought, *I still don't have any food.* Gratefully, my mind was faster than my mouth, and I thought about his query for a moment before I smiled and replied. This smile was matched by the broad grin on Boubacar's face.

I then proceeded to share with him something I had recently consumed from the scriptures. To this day, I do not remember what I said to him; I only remember his response. After listening attentively to my gospel thought, he slowly rubbed his tummy and said, "Mmmmmm." I remember laughing out loud to his unconventional reaction.

I have shared this story for many years because it triggers a deep reminder to me of the covenants I made in the temple to always nourish my body physically and spiritually. What a beautiful object lesson God has given us with our bodies! How often do you hunger? As I teach scores of young men every year in seminary, most respond, "It never goes away." I do not know too many hungrier things on this planet than teenage boys. They will sometimes gnaw on the desks in class.

So if your body hungers multiple times every day, shouldn't that tell you how often your spirit hungers for righteous things? Keep feeding the flames of faith! I know you will not have as much time to study the scriptures now as you did in the mission field, but people make time their enemy by saying there is never enough time. In all reality, people usually make time for the things they want the most. Show the Lord that He still matters in your post-mission life. Don't say there is no time for Him. Make time for Him! President Henry B. Eyring shared this beautiful insight.

There is another way to look at your problem of crowded time. You can see it as an opportunity to test your faith. The

Lord loves you and watches over you. He is all-powerful, and He promised you this: "But seek ye first the kingdom of God, and his righteousness; and all these things shall be added unto you" (Matthew 6:33).

That is a true promise. When we put God's purposes first, He will give us miracles. If we pray to know what He would have us do next, He will multiply the effects of what we do in such a way that time seems to be expanded. He may do it in different ways for each individual, but I know from long experience that He is faithful to His word.[6]

The vital spiritual calisthenics of consistent prayer and scripture study will keep you firmly on the straight and narrow path instead of lost in the fog leading to the great and spacious building. If you are in need of some help in adding variety to your scripture study, I would recommend Elder David A. Bednar's talk entitled "A Reservoir of Living Water."[7] He will provide you with some additional ways to study the scriptures that you might never have considered.

These spiritual calisthenics of personal prayer and scripture study will go a long way in helping you with challenges to your faith. In the Internet age, it will not be long before you will read something that calls our religion into question. Here are some of the biggest challenges I have noticed giving people in the Church spiritual heartburn:

- Women and the priesthood
- Blacks and the priesthood
- Same-sex attraction
- Gay marriage
- Plural marriage (polygamy)

How Can I Perform My Physical and Spiritual Calisthenics Daily?

- Multiple accounts of the First Vision
- Translation of the Book of Mormon
- The Book of Mormon and DNA
- The Book of Abraham
- Mountain Meadows massacre

This list is not exhaustive, but I think it is a good starting point. I would plead with you to give the Lord equal time. Do not become so immersed in studying from reputable scholarly sources that you forget the source of greatest repute: God. He is the only real source of truth and light. Give Him time for in His word to illuminate your understanding. Other sources might try to reflect light in an effort to illuminate truth, but often arguments against His divinely established Church end up failing to show the path that we should trod, "especially if one's real desire is to parade his discontent. Letting off steam always produces more heat than light."[8]

As you are doing the mental gymnastics necessary to try and solve your cognitive dissonance, be patient! God will answer, but it will be "in his own time, and in his own way, and according to his own will" (D&C 88:68). Visit www.lds.org. Many of these concerns have been addressed with refreshingly straightforward information from a faithful perspective. One of Satan's tactics is to stir people up to anger against God and His divine work.[9] Satan gets people angry about doctrine, and God has said: "Therefore they will not ask of me" (D&C 10:21). I know the Lord wants us to return to Him. Do not give up or turn in your membership if answers do not come sooner than you would hope.

10 Questions to Answer
after Serving a Mission

If you are traveling the lonely path of doubt, find solace in the fellowship of the desolate. You will not always walk with certainty, but you will always have a choice of where to define your faith.

> The call to faith is a summons to engage the heart, to attune it to resonate in sympathy with principles and values and ideals that we devoutly hope are true *and which we have reasonable but not certain grounds for believing to be true*. There must be grounds for doubt as well as belief, in order to render the choice more truly a choice, and therefore the more deliberate, and laden with personal vulnerability and investment. An overwhelming preponderance of evidence on either side would make our choice as meaningless as would a loaded gun pointed at our heads. The option to believe must appear on one's personal horizon like the fruit of paradise, perched precariously between sets of demands held in dynamic tension. Fortunately, in this world, one is always provided with sufficient materials out of which to fashion a life of credible conviction or dismissive denial.[10]

For those of you struggling with issues about the Church, take hope in knowing even Jesus's Apostles didn't fully understand His mission. They walked and talked with the Savior for three years and still did not fully grasp the meaning of His ministry. It was essential for Christ to perform the Atonement. It was a necessity, and a culmination of His time on earth. Even after teaching this to His Apostles, they still greatly mourned and sorrowed after the Crucifixion. It was not until Christ was resurrected and taught them for forty days did the Apostles truly start to see who the Savior was and what their role was now as His witnesses.

As one of the modern Apostles said, "Hold fast to what you already know and stand strong until additional knowledge comes."[11] Another Apostle reminded us to "doubt [our] doubts before [we] doubt [our] faith."[12] The only true source of knowledge is God. He giveth and he taketh away.[13] Perhaps you are troubled by some of the inconsistencies you see, especially in Church history. Please understand that there are reasonable explanations for each of these seemingly seismic blows to our faith. I have founded my faith upon the Rock of my Redeemer, and though the winds and the waves might crash against my foundation, I know He will not fail me.

The beautiful dedicatory prayer for the Kirtland Temple—which Joseph Smith said that he received by revelation—in D&C 109:55–56 (emphasis added) reads, "Remember the kings, the princes, the nobles, and the great ones of the earth, and all people, and the churches, all the poor, the needy, and afflicted ones of the earth; that *their hearts may be softened* when thy servants shall go out from thy house, O Jehovah, to bear testimony of thy name; that *their prejudices may give way before the truth*, and thy people may obtain favor in the sight of all." I honestly believe that you cannot have full access to all the light, power, and beauty of the Atonement of Christ unless you remain close to Him. And how can you remain close to Him without loyalty to His word,[14] prophet,[15] and Church?[16]

Adam provides us with the perfect example of what to do when we might be unsure of the future. After enjoying the beauties and spontaneous goodness of the Garden of Eden, Adam and Eve made the choice to leave—thus incurring the consequences of physical and spiritual death, as well as the future accumulation of sin. I can only imagine the difficulties of transitioning from paradise to the brutal reality of thorns, thistles, briars, and noxious weeds. Above all, I wonder how crushing the loneliness became outside, having only each other to rely on when they once walked and talked with God.

Then God "gave unto them commandments, that they should worship the Lord their God, and should offer the firstlings of their flocks, for an offering unto the Lord. And Adam was obedient unto the commandments of the Lord" (Moses 5:5). This story gets particularly fascinating when an angel appeared and asked Adam why he offered sacrifice. I feel Adam's reply has tremendous application to our lives. Adam told the angel, "I know not, save the Lord commanded me" (Moses 5:6). The angel then went on to teach that animal sacrifice is a similitude of the sacrifice of the Only Begotten Son.

I have often wondered how long Adam was obedient before he received that explanation. The text merely says it was "after many days" (Moses 5:6). The truth I want you to understand is that obedience will bring further light and knowledge. It might not come for many days, but as surely as we have a God who makes covenants and promises, He will give us the light and knowledge we need if we will patiently and obediently follow Him.

I want any who read this to know that I believe in Christ because I *choose* to believe. I sincerely think belief is a choice, while true faith is a gift from God. No one can prove to me with empirical evidence that Christ rose from the dead. I simply choose to believe that the tomb was empty on the third day. That choice to believe comes from a feeling I develop in my heart and mind as I study the words of those who were present when Christ rose from the dead. I believe He lives, and because He lives I will forever follow His divine mandate to follow Him. That single invitation is why I live the way I do, and though my path of discipleship is littered with sins, I will continue to repent and follow after my Master until I finish my journey to the celestial kingdom with my family. "Look unto me in every thought; doubt not, fear not" (D&C 6:36).

May the Lord bless you with the promised spiritual protection stated in 1 Nephi 15:24: "And whoso would hearken unto the word of God, and would hold fast unto it, they would never perish; neither could the temptations and the fiery darts of the adversary overpower them unto blindness, to lead them away to destruction." What powerful imagery! A warrior is not useful in battle without his sight.

The adversary wants to obscure our vision in any way possible. He will use truth to tell a lie. He will lie and use truth to back himself up. Satan will even use the philosophies of man interlaced with scripture to suit his devilish purposes. In this journey of life that sometimes becomes a battle, do not become blinded by worldly sophistries. Continually hold tight to the iron rod. I promise you that the mists of darkness will eventually dispel, revealing to you the Light of the World. And if you continue to hear mocking words from those pointing the finger of scorn at you either digitally or in person, remember the simple response Nephi gave to those in the strange building: "But we heeded them not."[17] I know you have tasted the fruit; now you simply need to remember how sweet it is[18] and continue partaking of "the love of God."[19]

Additional Readings

- Steven Aldana, *The Culprit and the Cure*
- David A. Bednar, "A Reservoir of Living Water," BYU Speeches, February 4, 2007
- David A. Bednar, "Understanding the Importance of Scripture Study," Ricks College Devotional, January 6, 1998
- David A. Bednar, "Ye Are the Temple of God," Ricks College Devotional, January 11, 2000
- David A. Bednar, *Increase in Learning*, *Act in Doctrine*, and *The Power to Become*
- Terryl Givens, "Letter to a Doubter," (see also his book entitled *The Crucible of Doubt*)
- Michael Ash, *Shaken Faith Syndrome*

Notes

1. L. Tom Perry, "The Returned Missionary," *Ensign*, May 2001.
2. From www.wikipedia.com.
3. Richard G. Scott, "How to Obtain Revelation and Inspiration for Your Personal Life," *Ensign*, May 2012.
4. David A. Bednar, "Ye Are the Temple of God," Ricks College Devotional, January 11, 2000.

5. David A. Bednar, "Understanding the Importance of Scripture Study," Ricks College Devotional, January 6, 1998.

6. Henry B. Eyring, "Education for Real Life," *Ensign*, October 2002.

7. David A. Bednar, "A Reservoir of Living Water," BYU Speeches, February 4, 2007.

8. Neal A. Maxwell, " 'Murmur Not,' " *Ensign*, November 1989.

9. See D&C 10.

10. Terryl Givens, "Letter to a Doubter," (fireside, October 14, 2012), http://terrylgivens.com/wp-content/uploads/2010/03/Letter-to-a-Doubter.pdf.

11. Jeffrey R. Holland, " 'Lord, I Believe,' " *Ensign*, May 2013.

12. Dieter F. Uchtdorf, "Come, Join with Us," *Ensign*, November 2013.

13. See Job 1:21.

14. D&C 18:33–36.

15. D&C 1:17–29; 21:1–6; 28:2–3, 6–7; 43:1–6.

16. D&C 1:30.

17. 1 Nephi 8:33.

18. 1 Nephi 8:10–12. Notice the adjectives used to describe the fruit: happy, joy, most sweet above all that I ever before tasted. Alma 32:35 described the taste as being light. See also Alma 36:24–26.

19. 1 Nephi 11:21–22.

Question 3

How Will I Make Worshipping the Lord at Church on Sunday a Priority?

"Partaking of the sacrament is the center of our Sabbath day observance."[1]
—*Elder L. Tom Perry*

SABBATH DAY OBSERVANCE is at the heart of the covenant God has made with man. After the creative periods were complete, God blessed the seventh (or Sabbath) day and sanctified it.[2] Israel would continually refer to the Sabbath as a day of rest, and laws were given from Moses about not working or laboring on the Lord's day. It is during the sacramental service that Christians would worship Christ by partaking of the emblems of His body and blood. This renewal and remembrance should be one of your highest priorities as a returned missionary.

You might be familiar with the phrase "the Sabbath has become a holiday instead of a holy day." I had one seminary student share with me that this day used to be called the Sabbath, then it was called Sunday, and now it is just called the weekend; another day off, a day to get stuff done, or a day to do whatever you want with your free time. The focus on us instead of God, whom we worship, seems to be the mantra of the world. We worship our creations or even His creations instead of the Creator Himself. That is the definition of idolatry, and instead of primitively bowing down to statues, we build up sophisticated electronic contraptions and pledge allegiance with all our time and attention. The dichotomy presented here is the difference between honoring covenants and indulging in covetousness.

Though the words look similar, they could not be more different. Covenants nurture a mutual relationship with the Lord while coveting feeds a craving for that which will ultimately yield moths and rust.[3] You know we cannot only be Sunday Mormons. Make sure you are not a one-day-a-week Latter-day Saint, who doesn't attend Sabbath services or who ward hops around, looking for the best fit. Let your heart and your membership be anchored in the ward you live in. Then you can truly begin to reap the full blessings of your covenant membership in the Church.

My parents were God-loving Latter-day Saints. My siblings and I were raised in a home where attending Church every Sunday was an expectation. My father and mother understood the Lord's instruction to parents in Doctrine and Covenants 68 about teaching children the gospel so that they could one day be fully responsible for their actions. I have students assert that their parents cannot make or force them to do religious things, especially going to Church, because they have agency. I try to teach them that while they do have agency, their parents have a covenant responsibility to God to ensure that they use their agency well. Then, when they leave the house, they will have unfettered access to their agency and power to act, and therefore be solely responsible and accountable for their own actions.

Now that you are an adult, I would encourage you to attend a single's ward, if possible, after returning from your mission. The worship and the activities are specifically geared toward your needs and age group. If you prefer a family ward, that is fine, but whichever you choose, be loyal to the structure that prophets and Apostles with priesthood keys have designed to help you "meet together oft, to fast and to pray, and to speak one with another concerning the welfare of [your] soul" (Moroni 6:5).

Sure, you can be edified attending a random LDS ward, but without your membership record, a bishop cannot extend you a calling or assign you home or visiting teachers.

As a young man, I used to think going to church was all Sunday was about. As I have matured in the gospel, I now realize that the Sabbath is the whole day, not just the three hours I spend at church. This means it is a day I should devote to God for His work and His purposes.

I really do not think God rested on the seventh day because he was tired. He is omniscient and omnipotent. I genuinely believe He set aside the Sabbath for us. We often get caught up in our lives with all the work we have to do: family, job, school, friends, and so on. Sunday is a day set aside to focus on Him since the "natural man"[4] has a tendency to forget. Therefore Christ taught, "The Sabbath was made for man, and not man for the Sabbath" (Mark 2:27).

There are two distinct parts to the physical church portion of Sabbath day worship. There is a personal and a social element.

How Will I Make Worshipping the Lord at Church on Sunday a Priority?

Elder Joseph B. Wirthlin taught that we need both a "spiritual conversation and a social integration"[5] to the Savior's gospel.

First, I will focus on the individual aspect of worship at church. How do you personally prepare for the Sabbath day? One Primary song teaches that Saturday is the day to get ready for Sunday. I smile when it is sung, but the principle is true. How well do you set yourself up for spiritual success on Sunday? How early do you wake up? What kind of music do you listen to in the morning before attending church? I laugh when I hear seminary students talk about how difficult it is to get up on Sunday when their services start at nine in the morning. My humor spills over to the observation I make with them about when school begins and how they amazingly seem to make it to school by seven or eight a.m. Please do not make your commitment to Sabbath worship more difficult by being up all night before. You can still stay out late and make it to your Sunday meetings early. It takes a willingness to make it a priority. Do not make the Church an enemy with your choices the night before.

A modern Apostle taught this idea quite forcefully:

> Our observance or nonobservance of the Sabbath is an unerring measure of our attitude toward the Lord personally and toward his suffering in Gethsemane, his death on the cross, and his resurrection from the dead. It is a sign of whether we are Christians in very deed, or whether our conversion is so shallow that commemoration of his atoning sacrifice means little or nothing to us.[6]

I watched this occur in my home ward a few years ago as I observed a sister partaking of the sacrament. This person had been restricted from attending church for a lengthy period of time because of health reasons. I do not know if she had the sacrament regularly administered to her in the home, but I distinctly remember watching her approach and partake of the emblems of the Lord's body. The intensity of her communion with God was absolutely beautiful. I could physically see on her face the power of the Atonement. Even though I intruded on a sacred moment, I was instructed by her example and the power of the Spirit. The importance of individual communion with God during this sacred ordinance cannot be achieved by anyone but yourself.

When you arrive at your church, how much time do you have to listen to the prelude music and attune you mind and heart to the messages you will receive? All the talks, prayers, and music play second fiddle to the importance of renewing your covenants with the Savior. The sacrament portion of the services is the most intensely personal part of any Sabbath worship. The chance to connect with God in an intimate way can never be minimized or overlooked in your life. Make sure this is a sacred, focused time for you to commune and even plead with the Lord for His atoning grace.

I remember a sacrament meeting in Idaho shortly after I came home from my mission, where we sang Hymn 169, "As Now We Take the Sacrament." I remember the feeling I had of wanting to be forgiven as I moved forward with the next part of my life. I continue to feel that same power as I worship from week to week in my ward. As you are sanctified during the sacrament, you will be better prepared to receive the messages God will give you through the Spirit during the rest of sacrament meeting.

How Will I Make Worshipping the Lord at Church on Sunday a Priority?

There is a deep meaning to renewing covenants on Sunday through the sacrament portion of our worship. Elder L. Tom Perry taught,

> The purpose of partaking of the sacrament is, of course, to renew the covenants we have made with the Lord.
>
> Elder Delbert L. Stapley instructed us in this when he said about covenants:
>
> "By partaking of the sacrament we renew all covenants entered into with the Lord and pledge ourselves to take upon us the name of his Son, to always remember him and keep his commandments (in Conference Report, October 1965, 14)."[7]

This suggests that we also renew our temple covenants when we partake of the sacrament. Elder Dallin H. Oaks also took the sacramental covenants deeper when he taught their connection to the temple.

> It is significant that when we partake of the sacrament we do not witness that we *take upon us* the name of Jesus Christ. We witness that we are *willing* to do so. (See D&C 20:77.) The fact that we only witness to our willingness suggests that something else must happen before we actually take that sacred name upon us in the most important sense.
>
> What future event or events could this covenant contemplate? The scriptures suggest two sacred possibilities, one concerning the authority of God, especially as exercised in the temples, and the other—closely related—concerning exaltation in the celestial kingdom.[8]

10 Questions to Answer after Serving a Mission

Rejoice with me in the fact that we have a God who makes covenants with us and who always keeps His promises. I was struck this last time reading through the Book of Mormon at how often the Lord taught that He is a god who fulfills the promises made in the past and remembers the promises made to His people. When we belong to Christ, He will love us, forgive us, and defend us.

Part of that defense comes from the social aspect of Sabbath worship. Christ teaches us to "take my yoke upon you, and learn of me; for I am meek and lowly in heart: and ye shall find rest unto your souls. For my yoke is easy, and my burden is light" (Matthew 11:29–30). The burden of discipleship is light because we do not have to do it alone. Not only has Christ paid the price of sin so we will not have to shoulder unbearable spiritual crosses, He also eases our physical burdens through other covenant members of the Church. So we are contractually obligated to "mourn with those who mourn, and comfort those who stand in need of comfort" (Mosiah 18:9).

I truly appreciate covenant-keeping Mormons! I have been blessed on numerous occasions by others fulfilling their obligations to the Lord by blessing me. Every child born to our family not only means a new bundle of joy to bring home, but it also brings to pass multiple meals served hot and fresh to our home. When we decided to move to another home within our own home ward, all I had to do was ask on Sunday and multitudes of elders with their trucks arrived on my doorstep at six p.m. to haul our belongings to another house. I even had two elders spend far more time than they needed to—late into the night—to take the final load to our new house.[9]

How Will I Make Worshipping the Lord at Church on Sunday a Priority?

Covenants bind us to Christ and also provide us with the opportunity to spread His love and mercy to others. Full access to His Atonement comes only as we keep our covenant promises to Him. Therefore, as a returned missionary, you are under a divine mandate to get a calling and continue your Church service to others. Your service will provide another witness to the reality of the gospel to other disciples of Christ in your ward. You can have just as sacred of experiences serving in your ward as you did on your mission if you will still serve "with all your heart, might, mind and strength" (D&C 4:2).

A friend of mine described it this way. We are both religious educators, and I have had the honor of teaching his two oldest daughters in seminary. He saw me one day at the seminary and said, "Look, the famous Brother White!" Sensing his praise as somewhat excessive, I smiled and shook his hand. He then went on to say I nearly walked on water in his house. I told him to stop being so dramatic, and he explained that his daughters often came home from seminary eager and excited to share what they had learned. They even quoted things I said in class. My friend then shared with me his astonishment as he said to his daughters, "I have been trying to tell you that for years!"

I call this the second witness principle. So during your service in the Church, especially with the youth, you will have experiences where you can teach gospel principles and bear powerful testimony to people who have heard these truths before, but now are receiving an additional witness from another source other than mom or dad. This additional witness is ratified in the heart by a third and most important witness: the Holy Ghost.

10 Questions to Answer
after Serving a Mission

Do not let others dictate how you worship the Lord at church. If you have not been offended at church, sooner or later you will have another Saint test your willingness to turn the other cheek. As members of the Church, we can be unkind at times while still trying to follow the Savior. Remember what Elder Bednar taught, "Believing that another person offended us is fundamentally false. To be offended is a *choice* we make; it is not a *condition* inflicted or imposed upon us by someone or something else."[10] One seminary student's mother shared with me that she left the Church for twenty years because she let other people's judgments control her. Instead of worrying about intentional or unintentional offense coming from imperfect people, resolve now to give them the benefit of the doubt. This includes your leaders, who will at times make mistakes as well.

One of the big disservices you can do to yourself while at Church meetings is allowing yourself to be distracted by a digital device. Distractions have always been a problem, but they seem to be more readily available now than ever. I have heard single adult ward bishops lament about seeing many in their congregations with their heads down, not communing with God but communicating with others—using their thumbs. Remember this principle that applies to every area of your life when you spiritually worship: If you are going to be in *holy* places, then be *wholly* there.[11] Do not just show up to Church physically. Give God your heart and your mind. There is a simple solution: set your phone to airplane mode so any extracurricular message "yields to the enticings of the Holy Spirit" (Mosiah 3:19).

How Will I Make Worshipping the Lord at Church on Sunday a Priority?

Elder Dallin H. Oaks spoke pointedly about such distractions while masterfully teaching about Christ's parable of the sower in Matthew 13:

> If the emblems of the sacrament are being passed and you are texting or whispering or playing video games or doing anything else to deny yourself essential spiritual food, you are severing your spiritual roots and moving yourself toward stony ground. You are making yourself vulnerable to withering away when you encounter tribulation like isolation, intimidation, or ridicule.[12]

Please take full advantage of the root-strengthening power that the sacrament and weekly worship service afford to your spirit so *when* (not *if*) the winds and storms of the adversary beat upon you, "it shall have no power over you to drag you down to the gulf of misery and endless wo, because of the rock upon which ye are built" (Helaman 5:12).

Outside of being offended or distracted, there is one other worry I have with Sabbath day worship in the Church. There could come a point as a returned missionary where you feel like you have learned all you need to know in the gospel. Therefore, going to church is not "fulfilling your needs" anymore. Beware of having such a selfish attitude. Even if you do not learn anything "new" in sacrament meeting, that does not mean you still cannot learn. If the Holy Ghost is the ultimate teacher, you can always be uplifted and edified. "If we come to be entertained, we often will be disappointed."[13]

President Spencer W. Kimball certainly understood this when he was asked by a member of the Church what he did when he was stuck in a boring sacrament meeting. His response is instructive: "I don't know. I've never been in one."[14] My take on this is that President Kimball understood this principle of being taught by the Holy Spirit.

Let's be honest in saying that there might be some classes that don't intellectually stimulate us, or there might be some talks we find as dry as the Sahara. At times like these, I hope that you will remind yourself of what you have to give to others at church instead of simply being a taker. Remember, covenant versus covetous. Though your sacrament worship is intimately personal, much of the other services are there to allow you to draw strength from others and to give help to those who desperately need love and compassion. I love Sister Bednar's example while she is at church. Elder Bednar took an opportunity to highlight a gift of the Spirit his wife possesses, which can be instructive for all of us.

> Before attending her sacrament meetings, Sister Bednar frequently prays for the spiritual eyes to see those who have a need. Often as she observes the brothers and sisters and children in the congregation, she will feel a spiritual nudge to visit with or make a phone call to a particular person. And when Sister Bednar receives such an impression, she promptly responds and obeys. It often is the case that as soon as the "amen" is spoken in the benediction, she will talk with a teenager or hug a sister or, upon returning home, immediately pick up the phone and make a call. As long as I have known Sister Bednar, people have marveled at her capacity to discern and respond to their needs. Often they will ask her, "How did you know?" The spiritual

gift of being quick to observe has enabled her to see and to act promptly and has been a great blessing in the lives of many people.[15]

The point of the Sabbath day is not just to serve others and get spiritual nourishment; it is also to get you clean. Scripturally, this means being holy. The word *holy* fascinates me because there is deep spiritual meaning to it. The Bible Dictionary defines *holiness* as "things or places . . . that were set apart for a sacred purpose. The opposite of holy is therefore common or profane."[14]

We do not just show up at church to put in our time because we have to. We are trying to become holy, like Christ. It is significant to note that another name for God the Father is "Man of Holiness" (Moses 6:57). Therefore, when Christ is referred to as the Son of Man in the New Testament, we see the frankly clear connection, with Him being the Son of the Man of Holiness. "The word *holy* . . . came to refer to moral character. Israel must be holy in character because the God of Israel was holy."[17]

The Lord's eternal promise to us is if we "offer up [our] sacraments upon [His] holy day," then we will "more fully keep [ourselves] unspotted from the world" (D&C 59:9). Sin is a spotted stain upon our souls. The principle I would have you remember is the better you keep the Sabbath day holy, the less likely you will take the stain of the world upon you. Doing what the world does on the Sabbath creates spots, and often those spots can bleed into the other portions of our lives. I have focused much of my writing in this chapter upon the physical church portion of your worship. But there is so much more. If your goal is to become holy and have that cleanliness seep into your character, you will find positive ways to keep the Sabbath instead of noticing all the limitations it places upon your time. *For the Strength of Youth* will give you some direction about a few of the things to do and not to do on the Sabbath, but ultimately what do you want your character to include: spots or holiness?

President Spencer W. Kimball elaborated further on Sabbath worship. He taught,

> The Sabbath is a holy day in which to do worthy and holy things. Abstinence from work and recreation is important, but insufficient. The Sabbath calls for constructive thoughts and acts, and if one merely lounges about doing nothing on the Sabbath, he is breaking it. To observe it, one will be on his knees in prayer, preparing lessons, studying the gospel, meditating, visiting the ill and distressed, writing letters to missionaries, taking a nap, reading wholesome material, and attending all the meetings of that day at which he is expected.
>
> One good but mistaken man I know claimed he could get more out of a good book on Sunday than he could get in attending church services, saying that the sermons were hardly up to his standards. But we do not go to Sabbath meetings to be entertained or even solely to be instructed. We go to worship the Lord. It is an individual responsibility, and regardless of what is said from the pulpit, if one wishes to worship the Lord in spirit and in truth, he may do so by attending his meetings, partaking of the sacrament, and contemplating the beauties of the gospel. If the service is a failure to you, you have failed. No one can worship for you; you must do your own waiting upon the Lord.[18]

How Will I Make Worshipping the Lord at Church on Sunday a Priority?

Ultimately, you are the one responsible for your Sabbath day worship. If you want to feel the power of the Savior's mercy and Atonement, lose yourself in the same kind of service on Sunday as you did in the mission field. You might not have seven days to give wholehearted service anymore, but you have at least one day where you can set aside your temporal cares and worries and gain access the sanctification that comes by yielding your heart to God.[19] Keep the Sabbath day holy, and you will find yourself led to the house of the Lord, where these words are inscribed on the edifice: "Holiness to the Lord."

Additional Readings

- For the Strength of Youth, "Sabbath Day Observance"
- *True to the Faith*, "Covenant," "Sabbath," and "Sacrament"
- L. Tom Perry, "The Sabbath and the Sacrament," *Ensign*, May 2011
- Dallin H. Oaks, "No Other Gods," *Ensign*, November 2013
- Spencer W. Kimball, "The Sabbath—A Delight," *Ensign*, January 1978
- Spencer W. Kimball, "The False Gods We Worship," *Ensign*, June 1976, (reprinted in the *Ensign*, June 2013)

Notes

1. L. Tom Perry, "The Sabbath and the Sacrament," *Ensign*, May 2011.
2. See Genesis 2:3; Moses 3:3.
3. See Matthew 6:19.
4. See Mosiah 3:19.

5. Joseph B. Wirthlin, "Restoring the Lost Sheep," *Ensign*, May 1984.

6. Mark E. Petersen, "The Sabbath Day," *Ensign*, May 1975.

7. L. Tom Perry, "As Now We Take the Sacrament," *Ensign*, May 2006.

8. Dallin H. Oaks, "Taking upon Us the Name of Jesus Christ," *Ensign*, May 1985.

9. Thanks very much, Johnny Tanner and Cody Erickson!

10. David A. Bednar, "And Nothing Shall Offend Them," *Ensign*, November 2006.

11. Thanks, Sister Kristy Dimmick, for sharing that profound one-liner with me.

12. Dallin H. Oaks, "The Parable of the Sower," *Ensign*, May 2015.

13. Donald L. Hallstrom, "Converted to His Gospel Through His Church," *Ensign*, May 2012.

14. Quoted in Donald L. Hallstrom, "Converted to His Gospel Through His Church," *Ensign*, May 2012.

15. David A. Bednar, " 'Quick to Observe,' " BYU Devotional, May 10, 2005 (reprinted in the *Ensign*, December 2006).

16. Bible Dictionary, "Holiness."

17. Ibid.

18. Spencer W. Kimball, "The Sabbath—A Delight," *Ensign*, January 1978.

19. See Helaman 3:35.

Question 4

How Will I Focus on Regular Worship at the Temple?

"The temple is the Lord's university."[1]

—*Sister Cheryl C. Lant*

TO THIS DAY, I can still clearly remember riding in my mission president's car over to the Denver Temple on my last full day in the mission field. A couple of the other missionaries and I were grilling President Thomas about what to expect when we went home and seeking his counsel about how to make the transition. His advice was brief but memorable. He told us, "Stay close to the temple." We naturally asked other follow-up questions but that was really all the wisdom he imparted to us that night.

I believe his words were the perfect counsel for me upon returning from a full-time mission, and I would recommend them to you. If you are frequenting the temple on a consistent basis, you are putting yourself in the house of the Lord. In His house, you can receive the revelation necessary to guide you during this time of huge decisions in your life. If your path to the temple is frequently traveled, I hope that means you are doing what is necessary to be worthy to enter the presence of the Lord.

I have heard the Brethren encourage members of the Church to participate in "regular" temple attendance.[2] But what does *regular* mean? Where you live could largely determine how often you attend the temple. Here is some help from the First Presidency in determining for yourself what regular temple attendance means.

> We are grateful for the increased availability of temples world-wide and invite adult members to have a current temple recommend and visit the temple more often. Where time and circumstances permit, members are encouraged to replace some leisure activities with temple service. . . .
>
> We request that local priesthood leaders encourage temple-worthy members to consider ways in which more frequent daytime temple attendance could occur. Home and visiting teachers may wish to arrange transportation for those who need it, particularly during the daytime.[3]

When I returned to BYU after my mission, I set a goal to be in the temple regularly. This was difficult at first because I did not have my own transportation. But I made the sacrifice to get there monthly, and when I got my first car, I set a goal to be there weekly until I could memorize everything I needed to know during the endowment.

I have also recently heard of a number of returned missionaries receiving a call almost immediately to be a temple worker. Think about how powerful an experience that could be for you! You would have a set time every week to go and serve not only your ancestors but also serve other temple patrons. You would immediately be asked to start memorizing the ordinances and

How Will I Focus on Regular Worship at the Temple?

prayers performed in that holy edifice. Having those sacred words frequently running through your mind would help "virtue garnish thy thoughts unceasingly" (D&C 121:45). I encourage you to ask your bishop if this would be a possibility for you, as your time and circumstances permit.

With a commitment to frequently go to the temple will come the fruits of temple service. As you surely discovered in the mission field, there is a joy and happiness that attends the saving of souls. Now you can continue to discover that feeling in the house of the Lord. Temple work is missionary work for the dead! Elder Marlin K. Jensen described some of these fruits:

> I can honestly say that the most spiritually mature and happy people I know are ardent temple-goers. There is good reason for that. It is in the temple that the full sweep of God's program for us is told and retold, each telling bringing greater understanding and commitment to living life His way. . . . A good test of how well we are doing in our quest to come unto Christ may be how we personally feel about the temple and our experiences there. *Temple* can be synonymous with *happiness* and *joy*.[4]

I love the temple! I love the peace and power that I feel within its walls. I love to pause as I walk out of the temple and take a deep breath—my physical reminder of the spiritual fresh air that I just breathed while communing with God. I also love the way we are taught from a divine source. I am so impressed with the new temple films used in the endowment ceremony. The variety we experience between films is instructive. I love to watch the different subtleties about how the characters are portrayed in it. The words and people are the same, but the feeling and emotion can continue teaching us more about the plan of happiness and our place in it.

I am a much better disciple of the Savior when I remember the covenants I have made with Him and tap into the "power from on high."[5] The promises God has given me and my family extend infinitely beyond those hallowed walls.

Part of the beauty of temple ordinances for me has come as I have pondered and felt the wonderful truth of the sealing ordinance. Joseph Smith described the bond that unites couples and families to God as being "welded"[6] to each other. President Henry B. Eyring taught, "There is nothing that has come or will come into your family as important as the sealing blessings."[7] The reason I wanted to receive my temple ordinances is because I wanted to be with my family forever, both the one I was born into and the one I began with my sweetheart in the Boise Idaho Temple.

I think that we talk so much about the power of this horizontal connection, linking with our families, that we miss the grander perspective available through the sealing power. We are not just uniting our families here on earth. Our Heavenly Father is providing a way to vertically unite our families eternally with Him! This is His plan, and He wants His children to be sealed to Him. Remember, we are not just sealed to our spouse, children, and extended family; we are being sealed to God. We are "peculiar,"[8] or *segullah*, meaning we are His special treasure, bought with a price.

Some of the worries that I encounter in class as a seminary teacher are frequently expressed in this way: "Brother White, if my parents are divorced, who am I sealed to?" Or, "If my parents get remarried to different people in the temple, who am

How Will I Focus on Regular Worship at the Temple?

I sealed to?" I think the simplest way to view this concern is to realize we are being sealed to God. If your parents have broken their sealing covenant, as a child you will certainly feel a loss. Children are always left with the short end of the stick with divorce. Yet the power of being a child of the covenant cannot be overstated. So even if your parents have not lived up to their covenants, you can still access the power of the Savior's grace through your own covenants.

When Christ came to America in 3 Nephi 20:26, He taught, "The Father having raised me up unto you first, and sent me to bless you in turning away every one of you from his iniquities; and this because ye are the children of the covenant." Notice that Christ came to this group of Nephites first because they were children of the covenant. Then He said the blessing of being a child of the covenant includes Him helping you turn away from iniquity. Elder Nelson said, "Children of the covenant become a strain of sin-resistant souls."[9] Never underestimate the power that is available to you because you are a covenant keeper who is sealed to both the family you came from and the family you hope to establish!

If you are often attending the temple as a returned missionary, I hope to offer you some suggestions about enriching your trips there. One of the ways you can this is with family history. Seeking out our ancestors has been associated with the Spirit of Elijah since he was the prophet who restored the sealing power in the Kirtland Temple. This was foretold to Joseph Smith in his bedroom at seventeen years old by Moroni, who quoted Malachi's last two verses in the Old Testament.

10 Questions to Answer
after Serving a Mission

The earth is utterly wasted at the Second Coming if the hearts of the fathers and children are not turned to each other in two ways. First, because, if not, then the binding power of covenants to link us to God and to each other will not have been established and have no efficacy to save us. Second, the entire purpose of the earth is to provide us an experience to obtain physical bodies and use those bodies to follow Christ. If nobody has made covenants with Him, then the purpose of the earth has been wasted. Destruction and futility. Well, that is not going to happen if we are committed to connecting to our ancestors (roots) and preparing for our future posterity (branches) by being sealed as families at the temple in the present.

The advances in family history in just the last few years should give you hope that you can participate. I heard one professional genealogist say family history is Facebook for dead people. The generations before us were supposed to get the information recorded. Our generation is charged with cleaning it up and getting it right. With the technology right at our fingertips, it is time to jump in and get your own family tree put together. If you are not sure where to begin, I would encourage you to find a family history consultant who can help you start.

The wealth of online information, including the RootsTech conferences, is quite astounding. At the 2014 conference, Elder Andersen gave the youth of the Church this invitation: "I want to challenge each of you to set a personal goal to help prepare as many names for the temple as baptisms you perform in the temple. Again, my challenge for you is to prepare as many names for the temple as you perform baptisms in the temple."[10] I think this invitation can easily be applied to endowed adults too. Prepare as many names for initiatory, endowments, and sealing ordinances as you are performing in the temple.

If you think you have a valid excuse for not doing your family history work, you are wrong—even if you have faithful LDS family members in your genealogy all the way back to the time of Joseph Smith on both sides of your family. There is still work to do! From my own personal research, all eight of my great grandparents were born and raised in the Church. My parents have served as full-time missionaries in the Family History Center in Salt Lake City. I have just about every excuse not to do my family history work, and yet when I engage in looking for ancestors on my side or my wife's side of the family, I have never been disappointed. If you have a prayer in your heart, like the many experiences you had in the mission field, the Lord will lead you to those who need their temple work performed. You will also be inspired along the way with the lessons you can learn from those who went before you.

Here are some of the divine blessings promised to you if you willingly "embark in the service of God"[11] for your kindred dead. First, from Elder Bednar,

> I invite the young people of the Church to learn about and experience the Spirit of Elijah. I encourage you to study, to search out your ancestors, and to prepare yourselves to perform proxy baptisms in the house of the Lord for *your* kindred dead (see D&C 124:28–36). And I urge you to help other people identify their family histories.
>
> As you respond in faith to this invitation, your hearts shall turn to the fathers. The promises made to Abraham, Isaac, and Jacob will be implanted in your hearts. Your patriarchal

blessing, with its declaration of lineage, will link you to these fathers and be more meaningful to you. Your love and gratitude for your ancestors will increase. Your testimony of and conversion to the Savior will become deep and abiding. **And I promise you will be protected against the intensifying influence of the adversary.** As you participate in and love this holy work, **you will be safeguarded in your youth and throughout your lives.**[12]

Elder Scott echoed these promises one year later in general conference:

Any work you do in the temple is time well spent, but receiving ordinances vicariously for one of your own ancestors will make the time in the temple more sacred, and even greater blessings will be received. The First Presidency has declared, "Our preeminent obligation is to seek out and identify *our own* ancestors."

Do you young people **want a sure way to eliminate the influence of the adversary in your life?** Immerse yourself in searching for your ancestors, prepare their names for the sacred vicarious ordinances available in the temple, and then go to the temple to stand as proxy for them to receive the ordinances of baptism and the gift of the Holy Ghost. As you grow older, you will be able to participate in receiving the other ordinances as well. I can think of no greater protection from the influence of the adversary in your life.[13]

I really believe there are tremendous blessings that come from doing family history work because proxy work uses technology for such a divine purpose. I imagine that, as a young adult, you are well connected on a number of digital platforms. If you

How Will I Focus on Regular Worship at the Temple?

are consistently using your technological skills to bring people unto Christ, think of the power and the protection that will create to avoid the destructive power of pornography and other digital evils. You will be providing access for another person to receive the eternal cleansing power of the Atonement and the gospel. The direct corollary between family history work and resisting the adversary is unmistakable. Plug into the power of your family covenants and unplug the temptation to titillate.

If you are looking to deepen your understanding of temple worship and the imagery and symbolism that is richly presented there, take some time to search it out. There are fantastic books written by faithful LDS scholars who have explored rites, rituals, and symbols throughout Christianity that can enlighten your mind. While not essential to having a meaningful temple experience, these writings can cognitively stimulate a level of thinking that will continue to impress your mind with the deep reverence and power contained within those sacred walls. I love the depth with which the Lord can teach us about His temple. Remember that, above any secular source, the Lord will teach you through His Spirit if you are willing to consistently ask, seek, and knock. I have learned that we *ask* through prayer, we *seek* through the scriptures, and we *knock* through our obedience.[14]

One of the symbols most instructive to me when I worship in the temple is the union between man and woman. First, there is the literal story of Adam and Eve and what happened in the Garden of Eden. We have a limited amount of knowledge from our scriptures and the temple about all that went on there. It has been suggested that even the fruit was merely symbolic.[15] Second, there is the instructive story of Adam and Eve where we can learn to apply to our own lives. One of these non-exe-getical interpretations is seeing the connection to Christ and ancient Israel. Frequently, the connection between the two is interpreted within the marriage covenant, with Christ as the bridegroom and the Church (or covenant Israel) as the bride.

If you can apply the above relationship to Adam (represent-ing Christ) and Eve (representing us) while you are worshipping in the temple, the symbolism can provide deep meaning and reflection for your life and marriage.[16] This is one of the many ways I have seen my own temple worship become enhanced with consistent attendance and willing study.

If you are not regularly going to the temple, I plead with you to come back the Lord's house. I am not at all ignorant of the mistakes that can and will be made upon returning from the mission field. Gratefully, the Lord also knows our fallen and flawed natures. After reminding us that no unclean thing should be permitted to pollute His house, the Prophet Joseph Smith, in his dedicatory prayer for the Kirtland Temple, said, "And when thy people transgress."[17] He said *when*, not *if*. Joseph's plea then gives us the key back to God's presence: "they may speedily repent and return unto thee, and find favor in thy sight, and be restored to the blessings which thou hast ordained to be poured out upon those who shall reverence thee in thy house."[18]

No matter what mistakes you make—grievous or minute—speedily repent. There is a difference between mistakes and will-ful rebellion. If a desire for discipleship continues to direct your life, let the renewing power of repentance restore you back to the presence of the Lord in His house. Don't delay meeting with your bishop if your sins could jeopardize a temple recommend.

How Will I Focus on Regular Worship at the Temple?

Additional Readings

- Boyd K. Packer, *The Holy Temple*
- James E. Talmage, *The House of the Lord*
- Richard G. Scott, "The Joy of Redeeming the Dead," *Ensign*, November 2012
- David A. Bednar, "The Hearts of the Children Shall Turn," *Ensign*, November 2011
- Richard G. Scott, "Temple Worship: The Source of Strength and Power in Times of Need," *Ensign*, May 2009
- Russell M. Nelson, "Children of the Covenant" *Ensign*, May 1995
- David B. Haight, "Temples and Work Therein," *Ensign*, November 1990
- Ed J. Pinagar, *The Temple: Gaining Knowledge and Power in the House of the Lord*
- Alonzo L. Gaskill, *Sacred Symbols*

Notes

1. Cheryl C. Lant, "The Steps to the Temple," *Ensign*, August 2009.
2. See Thomas S. Monson, "The Holy Temple—A Beacon to the World," *Ensign*, May 2011; Richard G. Scott, "Temple Worship: The Source of Strength and Power in Times of Need," *Ensign*, May 2009; Silvia H. Allred, "Holy Temples, Sacred Covenants," *Ensign*, November 2008.
3. "Letter from the First Presidency," March 2003 (reprinted in *Ensign*, March 2004).

4. Marlin K. Jensen, "Living after the Manner of Happiness," BYU Devotional, September 19, 1995 (reprinted in *Ensign*, December 2002).

5. D&C 38:32, 38; 105:11.

6. D&C 128:18.

7. Henry B. Eyring, "Families under Covenant," *Ensign*, May 2013.

8. 1 Peter 2:9; Exodus 19:5.

9. Russell M. Nelson, "Children of the Covenant" *Ensign*, May 1995.

10. Neil L. Andersen, RootsTech Family History Conference, Salt Lake City, February 8, 2014.

11. D&C 4:2.

12. David A. Bednar, "The Hearts of the Children Shall Turn," *Ensign*, November 2011; emphasis added.

13. Richard G. Scott, "The Joy of Redeeming the Dead," *Ensign*, November 2012; emphasis added.

14. J. Thomas Fyans, "'Draw Near unto Me,'" *Ensign*, November 1985.

15. Bruce R. McConkie, "Christ and the Creation," *Ensign*, June 1982.

16. Thank you, Alonzo Gaskill, for sharing your wealth of knowledge about symbolism to open my mind to this idea.

17. D&C 109:20–21.

18. D&C 109:21.

Question 5
How Will I Accomplish My Educational Pursuits?

"For members of the Church, education is not merely a good idea—it's a commandment."[1]

—*President Dieter F. Uchtdorf*

WHEN I FIRST came home from my mission, I had no idea what I wanted to do professionally for the rest of my life. I had ideas as a kid that I wanted to be a professional video game player or veterinarian because I love cats (don't hold that against me). As I grew into my teens, I just could not nail down what I wanted to do for a living. So my first year in college I took general education classes, knowing I had my entire mission to figure out a career. Well, when I arrived back at BYU after serving in Colorado, I was still as stumped as ever. I had heard about how great the business program was at BYU, so I took a bunch of those classes, but it was to no avail. Accounting was hard enough and economics broke my limited business savvy. I had to turn to other alternatives.

10 Questions to Answer
after Serving a Mission

After coming home, I had the honor of teaching at the MTC in Provo, Utah. I heard the job paid decent and, best of all, I would have the chance to continue feeling the missionary spirit on a daily basis. While I struggled to figure out what classes in school would lead me to a profession, I absolutely loved teaching the gospel. I finally realized I wanted to be a religious educator for a living. I needed to get a bachelor's degree in whatever field that I chose to be considered. Having enjoyed some of my psychology and family science classes, I proceeded forward, hoping to be employed full-time with the Church, with another plan to enter professional counseling if it did not work out.

The reason I share my story is because I know that many of you might not be sure about what to do for a career. Please realize it might take time to figure it all out. Do not be discouraged if you are unsure. Proceed with faith and, with the Lord's gentle guidance, you can figure it out. Whether you know for sure or not what you want to do for a living, "education is the key to opportunity."[2] Doors will be opened and pathways will become more clear if you have multiple options to choose from.

I grew up hearing President Hinckley teach forcefully about the value of an education. In one general conference, he said,

> You are moving into the most competitive age the world has ever known. All around you is competition. You need all the education you can get. Sacrifice a car; sacrifice anything that is needed to be sacrificed to qualify yourselves to do the work of the world. That world will in large measure pay you what it thinks you are worth, and your worth will increase as you gain education and proficiency in your chosen field.[3]

How Will I Accomplish My Educational Pursuits?

A dear friend of mine, who was a successful teacher at an institution of higher learning, loved her job. She had the opportunity to inspire many with her love of the subject and the gospel and family. Her only regret was not getting any advanced degrees in her field. She worked for over thirty years at the same university and, at times, watched her former students get advanced degrees and become her boss because they had the one thing she did not: further education. She was not bitter, just regretful of her own missed opportunity.

The scriptures teach us the doctrine of education. "And as all have not faith, seek ye diligently and teach one another words of wisdom; yea, seek ye out of the best books words of wisdom; seek learning, even by study and also by faith" (D&C 88:118). And earlier, the Lord commanded us to be instructed in all things that involve His kingdom and work. Some of those named include astronomy, geology, history, current events, and national and international affairs.[4] Being well educated allows us to better the communities we are part of and also help other people around the world.

I do not think the Lord has much of an opinion about how we choose to employed, so long as we can live the gospel and share that light with those around us. "Be smart. The Lord wants you to educate your minds and hands, whatever your chosen field. Whether it be repairing refrigerators, or the work of a skilled surgeon, you must train yourselves. Seek for the best schooling available. Become a workman of integrity in the world that lies ahead of you. I repeat, you will bring honor to the Church and you will be generously blessed because of that training."[5] The idea of advanced training did not come to me until after I was already happily employed as a religious educator.

A couple of years after I began teaching seminary, a fellow teacher asked me when (not *if*) I was going to get a master's degree. I asked him his opinion on the matter, and ideas began to germinate in my mind about continuing my education. Not only could I bless my family with more education, but I could possibly open doors for the future. I applied and was accepted into a program.

The master's program stretched me and demanded rigorous cognitive discipline. The classes were difficult and the writing load was heavy, but my spirit soared as I applied my new-found knowledge to bless others. Some of the greatest academic achievements in my life have come because of higher education.

To the returned sister missionaries, I hope you will strive for educational greatness. Once again, President Hinckley gives such inspiring council about education and specifically to the women in the Church.

> Find purpose in your life. Choose the things you would like to do, and educate yourselves to be effective in their pursuit. For most it is very difficult to settle on a vocation. You are hopeful that you will marry and that all will be taken care of. In this day and time, a girl needs an education. She needs the means and skills by which to earn a living should she find herself in a situation where it becomes necessary to do so.
>
> Study your options. Pray to the Lord earnestly for direction. Then pursue your course with resolution.

How Will I Accomplish My Educational Pursuits?

The whole gamut of human endeavor is now open to women. There is not anything that you cannot do if you will set your mind to it. You can include in the dream of the woman you would like to be a picture of one qualified to serve society and make a significant contribution to the world of which she will be a part.

I was in the hospital the other day for a few hours. I became acquainted with my very cheerful and expert nurse. She is the kind of woman of whom you girls could dream. When she was young she decided she wished to be a nurse. She received the necessary education to qualify for the highest rank in the field. She worked at her vocation and became expert at it. She decided she wanted to serve a mission and did so. She married. She has three children. She works now as little or as much as she wishes. There is such a demand for people with her skills that she can do almost anything she pleases. She serves in the Church. She has a good marriage. She has a good life. She is the kind of woman of whom you might dream as you look to the future.

For you, my dear friends, the sky is the limit. You can be excellent in every way. You can be first class. There is no need for you to be a scrub.[6]

My wife and mother are two of my best examples of women of faith and virtue who received their education and have made the world a better place because of it. My mother graduated from BYU with her bachelor's degree in teaching in 1968. She traveled with my father to California and raised a family of seven kids. After I was old enough to be in school, she decided to go back to school to be a beautician. I remember her cutting many people's hair in our kitchen as I grew up. Included in that group were many missionaries, whose hair she willingly cut for free. After my little brother was old enough to be in school, she finally had the opportunity to put her twenty-year-old degree to work in an elementary school classroom as a resource aid. My mother is such an example to me of using education within the home to bless the family and outside the home to bless others all around.

My beautiful wife received a bachelor's from BYU as well and walked at graduation while seven months pregnant with our first child. After the birth of our second child, an opportunity arose for her to fulfill a dream of her own. Keenan had danced all during high school and she had continued in college, where part of the degree she earned was in dance. In 2007, with encouragement from many around her, she opened her own dance studio with a group of twenty-seven dancers. She was the owner, teacher, costume designer, music editor, bookkeeper, tax preparer, choreographer, event planner, and recital organizer. We made it work so that I could be home with the kids while she went to teach dance.

As her studio grew, she finally was able to get her own space and design the studio to her liking. Even better, she has now cut back her teaching load and hires qualified teachers who are majoring in dance at BYU or Utah Valley University. Now she largely manages the studio from home with 110 little dancers as a successful small business owner. Most important to me, our three beautiful daughters have a place once a week to dance and explore the wonder of movement in an environment with wholesome music and modest attire.

How Will I Accomplish My Educational Pursuits?

If you are feeling like your past poor performance in school is holding your future hostage, let me tell you about one of my dear friends. He never fully applied himself academically during his teenage years. Though he graduated from high school, he did so with pretty marginal grades. As he prepared himself for a mission, he finally got serious about the important things in life. The mission envelope came and he was called to the beautiful country of Japan. Nobody was more surprised than he was. With a newfound respect for the trust the Lord was giving him, he embarked in the service with all his heart, might, mind, and strength.

Upon returning after honorably serving for two years, he realized he would have to put in his time at a junior college before he could move onto a respectable university. He went to work and got fantastic grades for two years before he transferred to BYU. While at BYU, he competed admirably in the business program and graduated with his bachelor's degree. With his sights set on the future, he immediately applied to various colleges to get his MBA. He ended up at Texas A&M and received his degree in business, with an emphasis in supply chain management. Before he graduated, he had multiple corporate suitors trying to court him for his newfound and hard-earned skills. At a time when many people were losing their jobs, he has multiple doors open for him for a career in the field of his choice.

No matter what your grades were in high school, decide what it will take for your dreams to become a reality, and then go to work to make it happen.

10 Questions to Answer
after Serving a Mission

Your temporal education is not the only one you should be concerned with right now—your spiritual education should still be of the utmost priority. "Your education will strengthen your service in the Church. A study was made some years ago that indicated the higher the education, the greater the faith and participation in religious activity."[7]

Please enroll in institute immediately! Institute is basically seminary for college kids. Even if you are not actively in school, you can still further your religious education. Institute.lds.org will show you the closest place you can begin filling in your week with spiritual activities.

President Thomas S. Monson has asked you to put institute at the top of your to do list.

> If you are a single college student, I ask you to make participation in institute a priority. Married students and other young adults are also welcome and encouraged to attend. Think of it. Friends will be made, the Spirit will be felt, and faith will be strengthened. I promise you that as you participate in institute and study the scriptures diligently, your power to avoid temptation and to receive direction of the Holy Ghost in all you do will be increased. Divine favor will attend those who humbly seek it. That is a promise which I leave with you.[8]

Institute can truly be a home away from home, a place to anchor your life while so many choices and temptations swirl around you.

Elder M. Russell Ballard made this observation about your religious education.

How Will I Accomplish My Educational Pursuits?

Whether you attend a Church school or not, whether you attend college or not, do not think that you are too busy to study the gospel. Seminary, institute, or religion classes will provide balance to your life and add to your secular education by giving you another opportunity to spend time studying the scriptures and the teachings of the prophets and apostles. There are four outstanding new courses that I would encourage every young adult to look into and to attend.

He then went on to link the power of your spiritual education with your future.

And don't forget that classes and activities offered at your local institute or through your young single adult ward or stake will also be a place where you can be with other young men and young women and lift and inspire one another as you learn and grow spiritually and socialize together. Brethren, if you will set aside your cell phone and actually look around a little, you may even find your future companion at the institute.[9]

Elder L. Tom Perry made a fascinating observation about the institute program that I hope will give you increased motivation to attend:

The Church periodically checks the pulse and measures the progress of the institute programs. This last year an institute study revealed the following: of those graduating from institute, 96 percent received temple endowments; 98 percent of those receiving their endowments had their marriages performed in the temple; 96 percent of the men graduating from institute served missions.[10]

10 Questions to Answer
after Serving a Mission

As a returned missionary, institute is a safe place to find those of your own faith to surround yourself with, those who desire to walk the path of discipleship.

My concluding counsel for this chapter is one of warning. "Wisdom is the principal thing; therefore get wisdom: and with all thy getting get understanding" (Proverbs 4:7). As you seek to obtain a greater understanding of the people and the world around you, be careful not to let it go to your head. Let your learning develop into wisdom.

What I mean is best summed up by the prophet Jacob: "When they are learned they think they are wise, and they hearken not unto the counsel of God, for they set it aside, supposing they know of themselves, wherefore, their wisdom is foolishness and it profiteth them not. . . . But to be learned is good *if* they hearken unto the counsels of God" (2 Nephi 9:28–29; emphasis added).

Your opportunities from advanced learning will likely yield the fruits of a much higher earning capacity. However, the combination of income and intelligence can be a deadly cocktail if devoid of faith. The word *if* is the most crucial word from the above scripture. *If* is such a daunting word. *If* is full of potential with all the possibilities for success or failure. *If* invokes the divine gift of our power to act. Our agency enables us to return to the presence of the Lord *if* we will allow His Atonement to transform us into beings of light.

Some people become far too brilliant for their own good and turn to their own smarts instead of relying upon the Lord. Others turn to the strength of their own wealth, trusting their dollars all the while being lulled into "carnal security" (2 Nephi 28:21). President Benson taught, "The two groups who have the greatest difficulty in following the prophet are the proud who are learned and the proud who are rich."[11] It can be difficult for some when their money or learning outstrips a simple servant of God. Be careful that the blessings of education and subsequent prosperity do not lead you to rise up in rebellion or apostasy.

Often the fine-twined lines or opportunities from learning created serious problems among the Nephites. "And the people began to be distinguished by ranks, according to their riches and their chances for learning" (3 Nephi 6:12). Let your bounty of riches and brilliance of learning turn your heart to God. "And he who receiveth all things with thankfulness shall be made glorious; and the things of this earth shall be added unto him, even an hundred fold, yea, more. And he who receiveth all things with thankfulness shall be made glorious" (D&C 78:19). Your gratitude and acknowledgement of the God who gives you all things will bless you instead of curse you. President Monson said,

> My counsel to returning missionaries and to each young person is that you should study and prepare for your life's work in a field that you enjoy, because you are going to spend a good share of your life in that field. I believe it should be a field that will challenge your intellect and a field that will make maximum utilization of your talents and capabilities; and finally, I think it should be a field that will provide you sufficient remuneration to provide adequately for a companion and children. Such is a big order; but I bear testimony that these criteria are very important in choosing one's life's work.[12]

10 Questions to Answer after Serving a Mission

Though I did fail in my attempt at majoring in business when at college, I can tell you the one piece of advice I do remember from a wealthy man giving a lecture I attended. He taught us that we should find a job that we love, and then find someone who will pay us to do it.

Let your hard work in education set the table for the rest of your life. If you have to work at a job you do not enjoy for a time to help make it to one you do enjoy, then be the best at your employment until you achieve your version of success. Make your dreams become a reality!

Additional Readings

- www.besmart.com
- Thomas S. Monson, "Decisions Determine Destiny," *Ensign*, November 1979
- Dieter F. Uchtdorf, "Two Principles for Any Economy," *Ensign*, November 2009
- Gordon B. Hinckley, "Rise Up, O Men of God," *Ensign*, November 2006
- Gordon B. Hinckley, "A Prophet's Counsel and Prayer for Youth," *Ensign*, January 2001
- Gordon B. Hinckley, "How Can I Become the Woman of Whom I Dream?" *Ensign*, May 2001
- Gordon B. Hinckley, "The Perpetual Education Fund," *Ensign*, May 2001
- Ezra Taft Benson, "Fourteen Fundamentals in Following the Prophet," BYU Devotional, February 26, 1980 (reprinted in *Liahona*, June 1981)

Notes

1. Dieter F. Uchtdorf, "Two Principles for Any Economy," *Ensign*, November 2009.

2. Gordon B. Hinckley, "The Perpetual Education Fund," *Ensign*, May 2001.

3. Gordon B. Hinckley, "A Prophet's Counsel and Prayer for Youth," *Ensign*, January 2001.

4. See D&C 88:77–80.

5. Gordon B. Hinckley, "A Prophet's Counsel and Prayer for Youth," *Ensign*, January 2001.

6. Gordon B. Hinckley, "How Can I Become the Woman of Whom I Dream?" *Ensign*, May 2001.

7. Gordon B. Hinckley, "Rise Up, O Men of God," *Ensign*, November 2006.

8. See institute.lds.org/quotes.

9. M. Russell Ballard, "The Greatest Generation of Young Adults," *Ensign*, May 2015.

10. L. Tom Perry, "Receive Truth," *Ensign*, November 1997.

11. Ezra Taft Benson, "Fourteen Fundamentals in Following the Prophet," BYU Devotional, February 26, 1980 (reprinted in *Liahona*, June 1981).

12. Thomas S. Monson, "Decisions Determine Destiny," BYU Devotional, November 6, 2005 (see also *Ensign*, November 1979).

Question 6

How Will I Continue to Work Hard Now That I Am Home?

"If you want to be happy this year in school, or on a mission, or in a marriage—work at it. Learn to work."[1]

—*Elder Jeffrey R. Holland*

I HOPE THAT you learned how to work hard on your mission. I remember how well I slept on my mission because I felt exhausted almost every day when bedtime arrived. One evening, while in Loveland, Colorado, Elder Strom and I were praying together before bed. He fell asleep while I was voice for us in the prayer. When I finished, I smiled and left him kneeling beside the bed. A short time later he awoke loudly complaining of a cramp in his leg. This was one humorous example of how physically fatigued you can get while laboring among the people you love and serve.

I want to draw your attention to *For the Strength of Youth*. It was reworked and released in 2012. All the topics in the previous edition were repeated in the newest version except for one new topic: work and self-reliance. This portion is a significant addition worth your time and attention. Notice the first

How Will I Continue to Work Hard Now That I Am Home?

sentence: "Work is honorable."[2] I fear, as a society, we glorify free time as the ideal. We "put in our time" instead of working hard so we can live for the weekend. Beware of such philosophy! Look at what the Lord taught Adam in Moses 4:25: "By the sweat of thy face shalt thou eat bread." Work is an eternal principle.

"Developing the capacity to work will help you contribute to the world in which you live."[3] Which do you want to become, a giver or a taker? A contributor or a mooch?

As a young man, I remember the many times at Church activities where I would look for opportunities to bum food off people. I watched a reenactment of my begging ways after Church a few years ago. One young man came into the young women's room after their lesson was over, knowing the teacher consistently brought treats to class. After inquiring about having some of their treats, the young woman's leader said that he was welcome to have some candy. I thought he would only take a single piece. Oh no, this young man proceeded to stuff two handfuls of candy into his pockets. With surprise on my face, I shouted his name and called him a mooch, much to the delight and laughter of his older brother. The name stuck and, from then on, I have called him such. To his overwhelming credit, I have closely watched this boy turn into a hardworking, no complaints young man. I am impressed with his dedication to work, even if the affectionate nickname Mooch has remained. He is seeing the promise of hard work bring "an increased sense of self-worth"—think of how your hard work on your mission "bless[ed] you and your family."[4] Your continued commitment to laboring will do the same for you "now and in the future."[5]

10 Questions to Answer after Serving a Mission

"Learning to work begins in the home."[6] Though you likely do not live at your parents' home anymore, this principle can still be instructive. Think of the different chores and tasks you were expected to do growing up. How happy were you to help around the house? "Help your family by *willingly* participating in the work necessary to maintain a home."[7] The word *willingly* makes all the difference! Apply this to your immediate circumstances. If you have any roommates, willingly do your part to make your apartment or condo or house become a place where the Spirit can reside. Everyone needs to do their part. Do not get so caught up with the specifics that contention enters into the equation.

When my oldest two children are helping pick up around the house, I sometimes hear them complain, "But I didn't make this mess!" They are quick to point out their younger siblings as the culprits. I try hard, with love and patience, to point out how much Mom and Dad clean up around the house, especially when most of the messes are not our own. I then ask my older children if they will help the younger children clean up since they are more capable. To their credit, they are often willing to comply.

My encouragement to you is to learn how to be more willing now in your work around your residence because those good habits can follow you into your marriage. My wife is a brilliant cook. Her meals are as appetizing as she is wonderful. Therefore, after the meal is over, I take my turn in cleaning all the dinner mess until it is finished. I do this willingly because I appreciate her and all the time and effort she spends to nourish our family. Remember, "The Lord requireth the heart and a willing mind;

and the willing and obedient shall eat the good of the land of Zion in these last days" (D&C 64:34).

Your skills with managing your money well will go a long way in creating a happy and successful home in the future. Learn early to handle your money wisely and live within your means. Here is the definition of living within your means from lds.org: "Spending less money than you make is essential to your financial security."[8] It is critical to understand right now in your early adulthood the difference between needs and wants. Just because you want to eat out often does not mean your wallet would agree. This kind of thinking demands discipline.

The companion principle to living within your means is avoiding debt. The teachings of our latter-day prophets about this matter are clear and can be found in a multitude of sources. But you may wonder about acquiring debt to purchase certain big-ticket items. Again, from lds.org, "Avoid debt, with the exception of buying a modest home or paying for education or other vital needs. If you are in debt, pay it off as quickly as possible."[9] Remember that once you incur debt, interest is your constant companion until you free yourself from its bondage.

But what about credit cards? Isn't it important to build up a good credit score? While true, understand that credit can be a wonderful servant or a terrible taskmaster. Make your credit cards serve you instead of the other way around. I have known people who had to perform "plastic surgery" by cutting up their credit cards when the spending got out of control.

The 2009 Worldwide Leadership Training in the Church was devoted to the basic principles of welfare and self-reliance. I would highly recommend reading its contents. The material presented is available in a booklet from the Church or online.[10] Elder Robert D. Hales had some profound instruction on the topics of money and debt.

> [Provident living] means joyfully living within our means and preparing for the ups and downs of life so that we can be ready for the rainy-day emergencies when they come into our lives.
>
> Provident living means not coveting the things of this world. It means using the resources of the earth wisely and not being wasteful, even in times of plenty. Provident living means avoiding excessive debt and being content with what we have.
>
> We live in an age of entitlement. Many believe they should have all that others have—right now. Unable to delay gratification, they go into debt to buy what they cannot afford. The results always affect both their temporal and spiritual welfare.
>
> When we go into debt, we give away some of our precious, priceless agency and place ourselves in self-imposed servitude. We obligate our time, energy, and means to repay what we have borrowed—resources that could have been used to help ourselves, our families, and others.
>
> As our freedom is diminished by debt, increasing hopelessness depletes us physically, depresses us mentally, and burdens us spiritually. Our self-image is affected, as well as our relationships with our spouse and children, with our friends and neighbors, and ultimately with the Lord.
>
> To pay our debts now and to avoid future debt require us to exercise faith in the Savior—not just to *do* better but to *be* better. It takes great faith to utter those simple words, "We can't afford it." It takes faith to trust that life will be better as we sacrifice our wants in order to meet our own and others' needs.

How Will I Continue to Work Hard Now That I Am Home?

I testify that happy is the man who lives within his means and is able to save a little for future needs. As we live providently and increase our gifts and talents, we become more self-reliant. Self-reliance is taking responsibility for our own spiritual and temporal welfare and for those whom Heavenly Father has entrusted to our care. Only when we are self-reliant can we truly emulate the Savior in serving and blessing others.[11]

Two final thoughts about money. First off, beware of get-rich-quick schemes and philosophies. Almost every success story you hear about a person rising to wealth also includes the hard work they put into getting there. I worry about the idea of making all the money I can quickly, and then indulging for the rest of my life in doing whatever I want. Think about this for a minute. What would you do if you were somehow given ten million dollars right now? If I were to receive such a large windfall, I would continue with my current employment—not because I need the money anymore, but because of the internal satisfaction that comes from bringing souls unto Christ. I know a large sum of money could provide many temporal luxuries into your life immediately; however, possessions do not begat true happiness.

Laman and Lemuel missed this point when they fallaciously stated, "These many years we have suffered in the wilderness, which time we might have enjoyed our *possessions* and the land of our inheritance; yea, and we might have been *happy*" (1 Nephi 17:21; emphasis added). Contrast their lament with Nephi's attitude of seeing the distinct blessings from the hand of the Lord. Nephi's family also waded through the same trails and afflictions in the wilderness, yet he points out that they lived on raw meat and had the light of God to lead them to the promised land.[12] The Savior teaches a profound truth about our values in Matthew 6:21: "For where your treasure is, there will your heart be also."

Second, start up a budget now. Elder Hales taught,

> Preparing for the future includes making a spending and savings plan with our income. Carefully making and keeping a family or personal budget can help us recognize and control the difference between our wants and needs. Reviewing that budget in a family council will allow our children to learn and practice wise spending habits and to participate in planning and saving for the future.[13]

Early in our marriage, I took care of the finances for our family. After being hired as a seminary teacher, my wife volunteered to take on that responsibility. She had taken a money management course in college and wanted to relieve me of worrying about our income. I have been incredibly impressed with the way our family is blessed by her willingness to track our expenditures. She has said on more than one occasion that it is easy for her to spend money yet her discipline to live within our means continues to keep our home firmly anchored to the Rock that matters most.

What are your goals now and for the future? In chapter eight of *Preach My Gospel*, you were taught the importance of not just scheduling your time, but also actually planning for success. A friend of mine who has served as a stake president and mission president shared with me one of the laments he saw happen with returned missionaries. He indicated to me that many of the returned missionaries he interacted with often quit setting goals.

My hope for you is that you will plan for future success by setting short-term and long-term goals in all areas of your life: spiritual, physical, educational, personal, and so forth. Have weekly, monthly, yearly, and even a multi-year plans for your life. "Set high goals for yourself, and be willing to work hard to achieve them."[14] You learned how to be dependable and developed self-discipline on your mission. Do not let those habits go to waste!

Remember what the Lord told Moses: "I have a work for thee, Moses, my son" (Moses 1:6). Put your name in that verse and read it again. God has a work for *you* to do, and I promise that hard work will be part of it. The Lord knows what you are capable of with the gifts He has given you. Seek His guidance as you work to achieve your goals.

One way that you can seek the Lord's guidance is through studying the three places in scripture that list gifts of the Spirit: 1 Corinthians 12–13, Moroni 10, and Doctrine and Covenants 46. You will notice in your study that the Lord does not give every gift to any single individual, but "to every man is given a gift by the Spirit of God" (D&C 46:11). Therefore, we all at least have one gift.

The Lord also instructs us to "seek ye earnestly the best gifts" (D&C 46:8). He is inviting us to ask for gifts of the Spirit as long as we remember these gifts are "for the benefit of the children of God" (D&C 46:26). Any gift God has given you is to bless, not impress. I will often ask my seminary students if they could have one super power, what would it be? Many share the desire to fly, have incredible strength, or run super fast. One young woman in class then brought everyone back to earth with her truly humble response, "I would want to heal people." She clearly understood the Christian imperative that "it is more blessed to give than to receive" (Acts 20:35). Our godly gifts invite us to serve and be selfless, not be selective and selfish.

We all have at least one gift of the Spirit, but the Lord welcomes us to ask and seek for more gifts of the Spirit. We will be blessed with more if we remember the reason they are bestowed and give credit to Him who grants them. Paul concluded his great discourse about this topic by listing a bunch of spiritual gifts we can obtain. Yet, as a child of God, if I "have not charity, I am become as sounding brass, or a tinkling cymbal" (1 Corinthians 13:1). In essence, I think Paul is saying if we have all these gifts from God but are not willing to love others, we are nothing but a big noise. Cymbals and trumpets easily catch people's attention and can promote a "me" attitude. Be prepared to seek the Lord's help in achieving your goals and remember to love people and use things, not use people and love things.

As a young man of fifteen, I set some of the first spiritual goals of my life. I was highly influenced by a young woman two years older than me, who encouraged me to write them down and do everything that I could to achieve them. I still have the paper I wrote them on to this day. Twenty spiritual goals written out one night after a phone conversation about how cool it was to follow Jesus Christ and live my standards.

Before that conversation, I did not always think goals or hard work were cool. In fact, I used to have a keychain with a contemporary cartoon character saying, "Underachiever. And proud of it, man!" My mom expressed dismay at my having this. I did not think it was a big deal until my discipleship with the Savior demanded renunciation of such a foolish philosophy.

"The Lord has commanded us not to be idle."[15] I used to get the words *idle* and *idol* confused. An *idol* is a noun, meaning an object we worship; *idle* is most frequently used as an adjective or verb, meaning doing nothing. If the Lord has a work for you to do, of course He would command you not to be idle. Think of a car idling. The engine might be running, but it is not going anywhere. A few of reasons God commands us not to idle away our time is because "idleness can lead to inappropriate behavior, damaged relationships, and sin."[16] As much as I enjoy sharing stories, I will refrain from incriminating myself or any of my friends at this point. Speaking specifically to the men, think of a time when you and your friends were bored. Did your ideas of what to do sometimes lead you to inappropriate behavior? Exactly.

Another warning about idleness cautions against "spending excessive amounts of time in activities that keep you from productive work."[17] You will have to be honest with yourself to determine what "excessive" means to you. Such activities could include "using the Internet, playing video games, and watching television."[18] Obviously, technology is not inherently evil in and of itself. Yet we can become a slave to its almost gravitational pull. Remember, electronics are tools in your hand. This almost becomes a decision of what is good, better, or best.[19]

Early in our marriage, before any of our children arrived, I enjoyed indulging in what I thought was harmless video game playing. When all my perceived work was done, I would play because it was a release, and I did enjoy it. What I did not perceive was the effect that my gaming consumption was having on my young bride. She longed for more engaged interaction from me while I mindlessly droned on with my games. After a tearful discussion one night, I realized that "harmless" hobby was not as innocuous as I once believed. I made a decision to make my marriage more of a priority, which meant sacrificing some of what I wanted for what was better for us.

This, I feel, is an important transition in life. As individuals, we go from being dependent in our first family to being independent on our own to becoming interdependent when we marry. My relationships with my wife and children are much better because of this decision I made.

My favorite quote about avoiding idleness and being a hard worker comes from President Gordon B. Hinckley. He taught,

> I believe in the gospel of work. There is no substitute under the heavens for productive labor. It is the process by which dreams become realities. It is the process by which idle visions become dynamic achievements.
>
> Most of us are inherently lazy. We would rather play than work. We would rather loaf than work. A little play and a little loafing are good. But it is work that spells the difference in the life of a man or woman. It is stretching our minds and utilizing the skills of our hands that lifts us from mediocrity.[20]

What a fantastic concluding sentence! After all, no one wants to live a mediocre life.

So the converse of productive work would be gambling. We are counseled, "Do not waste your time and money in gambling. Gambling is wrong and should not be used as a form of entertainment. It is addictive and can lead to lost opportunities, ruined lives, and broken families."[21] Gambling teaches many phony philosophies, including that it is fun and harmless. It also teaches that you can get a lot of money quickly for relatively little effort. Be careful of these deceptive philosophies! Remember, "It is false to believe you can get something for nothing."[22]

Now, some would argue that Christ's Atonement gives us the free gift of the resurrection through no effort on our part in this mortal life. Remember that you still had to be willing to come here from premortal life to qualify for this beautiful gift. You had to keep your first estate.

President Gordon B. Hinckley gave a landmark talk on gambling in the April 2005 general conference. In this thorough address, the prophet shot down any argument that has been made to justify gambling. He even quoted seven other prophets and Apostles who have denounced gambling, adding additional witnesses to his testimony. Some of his best counsel is included in these statements:

> Gambling is simply a process that takes money and does not offer a fair return in goods or services. . . .
>
> One of our young men recently said, "Pay five bucks to see a movie; pay five bucks to play poker—it is the same idea." It is not the same idea. In one case you get something for which you pay; in the other case, only one picks up the winnings and the others are left empty-handed. . . .
>
> The pursuit of a game of chance may seem like harmless fun. But there attaches to it an intensity that actually shows on the faces of those who are playing. And in all too many

cases this practice, which appears innocent, can lead to an actual addiction. The Church has been and is now opposed to this practice. If you have never been involved in poker games or other forms of gambling, don't start. If you are involved, then quit now while you can do so. There are better ways to spend one's time. There are better pursuits to occupy one's interest and energy. . . .

Please, please do not fritter away your time or your talents in an aimless pursuit. If you do so, it will lessen your capacity to do worthwhile things. I believe it will dull your sensitivity to your studies in school. It will disappoint your parents, and as the years pass and you look back, you will be disappointed with yourselves.[23]

I remember one young man I taught in seminary inviting me to be part of his friends' March Madness basketball pool. I regularly fill out a bracket and compare it with my coworkers, family, and friends for fun, so I gladly accepted the invitation. Then I learned the catch. "It's only five dollars, Brother White." After telling the student I would not be joining them, he asked why not. I tried to explain that what he was doing was gambling, but he brushed off my comment with a simple, "It's only five dollars." I could see I was not going to persuade this young man, so I left the matter alone.

It was shortly after this experience that President Hinckley gave his gambling talk. While we discussed our favorite conference talks in class, the gambling issue came up. Both this young man and I smiled as he sheepishly admitted that he had learned a lesson.

How Will I Continue to Work Hard Now That I Am Home?

A contrast to the principle of gambling has been presented to me in the form of my good father. I will forever be grateful for his example when it comes to working hard. My dad moved his young family to the San Francisco Bay Area for employment shortly after graduating from BYU. After years of service, he was laid off during the recession in the late 1980s. After bouncing between a few jobs, he finally settled on the job he would have until retirement. I watched him work the night shift for the better part of twenty years at a job he was overqualified for. To help make ends meet, he would frequently accept substitute teaching assignments and come home after an eight-hour night shift to sub in a classroom of junior high students for another eight hours.

As a teenager, I was never left wanting, yet I had little idea about how much my parents sacrificed to raise seven children on such a tight budget. As a father of five now, I understand the demands my father went through to provide for us. This silent lesson of my stalwart father was not lost on me.

My parents are my best examples of self-reliance. "When you are self-reliant, you use the blessings and abilities God has given you to care for yourself and your family and to find solutions for your own problems."[24] Though we sometimes have an attitude in the Church of always wanting to help others—yet being reticent to accept it in return—"self-reliance does not mean that you must be able to do all things on your own."[25] We need to be able to accept help as well as be willing to give it.

I learned this particular lesson while I serving as a missionary in Grand Junction, Colorado. In addition to our local ward, my companion and I were assigned a small branch about one hour east of the city. While teaching a discussion to an older couple in the city of Collbran, we realized we had spent more time with this family than anticipated. With a long drive back to our apartment looming, we finished our discussion and prepared to leave.

The sweet sister we were teaching then had her own realization, which was that we did not get to eat dinner because of the length of our lesson. She immediately reached into her purse and produced a twenty and asked us to use it to eat dinner at the local diner on our way back to Grand Junction. Of course, as missionaries, we flatly refused to take the money, with the humble excuse that we would be fine. She insisted we take the money, and we again declined, this time with the excuse that we just could not take another person's money. Finally—and quite indignantly—she declared, "Will you deny me the blessing of feeding the servants of the Lord? The laborer is worthy of his hire?" (A reference to Luke 10:7.) With mouths hanging slightly open in awe and without a single logical way to refute her claim, my companion bowed his head and opened the palm of his hand.

This terrific sister taught me an incredibly valuable lesson that day. Acceptance of someone else's willing offering not only blesses the receiver but also the provider with additional divine blessings for his or her service.

Do not be afraid of hard work. But do also keep in perspective the things you are working to achieve. Remember, "The most important of the Lord's work you will ever do will be within the walls of your own homes."[26] As hard as I work to be a faithful religious educator, I must not let that take priority over my family. They deserve my best instead of my leftover time and effort. I truly believe that as you embrace the principle of hard work in your employment, you can measure your real success in the workplace with the level of commitment you have to your family.

Additional Readings

- *For the Strength of Youth*: "Work and Self-Reliance"
- *Basic Principles of Welfare and Self-Reliance*, The Church of Jesus Christ of Latter-day Saints
- *All Is Safely Gathered In* and *Family Finances and Family Food Storage*, The Church of Jesus Christ of Latter-day Saints
- Robert D. Hales, "Becoming Provident Providers Temporally and Spiritually," *Ensign*, May 2009
- Jeffrey R. Holland, "Living After the Manner of Happiness" BYU–Idaho Devotional, September 23, 2014
- Dieter F. Uchtdorf, "Two Principles for Any Economy," *Ensign*, November 2009
- Randell L. Ridd, "Work—Who Needs It?" *New Era*, July 2014
- Gordon B. Hinckley, "Gambling," *Ensign*, May 2005

Notes

1. Jeffrey R. Holland, "Living after the Manner of Happiness" BYU–Idaho Devotional, September 23, 2014.
2. *For the Strength of Youth: Fulfilling Our Duty to God* (Salt Lake City: Intellectual Reserve, 2012).
3. Ibid.
4. Ibid.
5. Ibid.
6. Ibid.
7. Ibid.

8. "Family Finances," lds.org.

9. Ibid.

10. https://www.lds.org/manual/basic-principles-of-welfare-and-self-reliance/a-gospel-vision-of-welfare-faith-in-action?lang=eng.

11. Robert D. Hales, "A Gospel Vision of Welfare: Faith in Action" in *Basic Principles of Welfare and Self-Reliance*.

12. See 1 Nephi 17:2–3, 12–13.

13. Robert D. Hales, "A Gospel Vision of Welfare: Faith in Action."

14. *For the Strength of Youth*.

15. Ibid.

16. Ibid.

17. Ibid.

18. Ibid.

19. Dallin H. Oaks, "Good, Better, Best," *Ensign*, November 2007.

20. Gordon B. Hinckley, *Teachings of Gordon B. Hinckley* (Salt Lake City: Deseret Book, 1997), 705.

21. *For the Strength of Youth*.

22. Ibid.

23. Gordon B. Hinckley, "Gambling," *Ensign*, May 2005.

24. Ibid.

25. Ibid.

26. Harold B. Lee, *Teachings of Harold B. Lee* (Salt Lake City: Bookcraft, 1988), 280.

Question 7

How Am I Striving to Create a Celestial Marriage?

"You have an important responsibility in choosing not only whom you will date but also whom you will marry."[1]

—*President Thomas S. Monson*

THIS TOPIC SEEMS to give a number returned missionaries a bit of angst. From my observations, most missionaries coming home fall into one of two groups. Either they quickly transition back into the dating and relationship scene, or they are still awkward about making small talk about nearly anything other than religion with strangers of the opposite sex.

I know you feel plenty of pressure to tie the knot. All those people who were hounding you about a mission before you went are now the people who will be nagging you about finding an eternal companion.[2] I hope that I can give you some hope for the immediate future and vision for the long term.

First of all, do not fear the next saving ordinance in your life. But you should not feel pressured to get married immediately. President Monson so practically taught,

10 Questions to Answer
after Serving a Mission

I should like to dispel one rumor that is very hard to put to rest. I know of no mission president in all the world who has ever told a missionary that he had the responsibility to marry within six months after his mission. I think that rumor was commenced by a returned missionary, and if not by a returned missionary, by the girlfriend of a returned missionary.[3]

He then continues by counseling you to lift your eyes. "I would admonish you to maintain an eternal perspective. Make certain that the marriage in your future is a temple marriage. There is no scene so sweet, no time so sacred as that very special day of your marriage. Then and there you glimpse celestial joy. Be alert; do not permit temptation to rob you of this blessing."[4]

Remember in the mission field those investigators who had such a difficult time making the commitment to be baptized? They often either lacked the faith to move forward or were held captive with their fears of what others would say. Do not make their mistake. If getting sealed for time and all eternity is the next ordinance available to you in your life, then actively pursue it with an attitude of faith! This does not mean you have to act desperate or become fanatical. You are not trying to marry the temple—you are trying to qualify for the blessings of exaltation with someone who chooses that as well.

I am fascinated that the temple sealing is the only saving ordinance that requires two people's agency. All other ordinances are made between an individual and God. Soon, three of you will be involved and have to make a covenant with each other.

It is not enough to just get married in the temple. Sometimes our LDS culture wrongly assumes that if your marriage is performed in the temple, then happily ever eternity is attached to it. Elder Robert D. Hales taught the difference between a temple marriage and a celestial one: "*Temple marriage* describes the place you go to have the marriage performed. *Celestial marriage* is being true to the sacred covenants you make in that temple marriage ceremony—living celestial principles in the marriage relationship."[5]

Therefore, you can have a temple marriage but not a celestial one. You must understand that the Holy Spirit of Promise will only stamp His seal of approval on a marriage that has made the right covenants in the temple but also enters into them outside the temple over the course of a lifetime.[6]

President Monson then rightful counsels,

> You have an important responsibility in choosing not only whom you will date but also whom you will marry. President Gordon B. Hinckley admonished: "Your chances for a happy and lasting marriage will be far greater if you will date those who are active and faithful in the Church." . . . It is essential that you become well acquainted with the person whom you plan to marry so that you can make certain you are both looking down the same pathway, with the same objectives in mind. It is ever so significant that you do this.[7]

I know of many young women in the Church who have a goal to marry a returned missionary. I would only add one small caveat to that goal, which is to marry someone who is converted to the Savior and is still willing to walk the road of discipleship. For the women, be sure that he not only served a mission, but that he is willing to serve the Savior for a lifetime. Don't marry returned missionaries just because they "put in their time." Make sure the changes that occurred from the mission are still bearing the fruits of "faith, virtue, knowledge, temperance, patience, brotherly kindness, godliness, charity, humility, diligence."[8]

You have likely been in a young men's or women's class where the topic was preparing for a temple marriage. In the end, it seems as if we make lists of what we want in a future spouse. Elder Bednar turned this thinking on its head quite forcefully. When it comes to making a list of demands about our future eternal companion, he said,

> You are so arrogant to think that you are some catch and that you want someone else who has these five things for you. If you found somebody who had these three or four or five characteristics you are looking for, what makes you think they'd want to marry you? The list is not for evaluating someone else. The list is for you, for me and what I or you need to become. And so if there are three primary characteristics that I hope to find in an eternal companion then those are the three things I ought to be working to become. Then it will be attractive to someone who has those things. So my advice is, you're not on a shopping spree looking for the greatest value with a series of characteristics. You become what you hope your spouse will be and you'll have a greater likelihood of finding that person.[9]

I love how this principle of becoming what you are hoping to find gives you the control when you are seeking someone to spend eternity with. Now, instead of being held hostage, waiting for Mr. or Ms. Right to show up, you can become what you are looking for. Birds of a feather flock together. You attract what you are. You are much more likely to find someone who is more similar to you than different from you. This is taught in D&C 88:40, which reads, "For intelligence cleaveth unto intelligence; wisdom receiveth wisdom; truth embraceth truth; virtue loveth virtue; light cleaveth unto light."

As you continue to become more like the Savior and seeking someone who also wants to make that beautiful journey through life with you, I hope I can give you some practical and spiritual counsel about how to do it. I find great wisdom and comfort in turning to the words of our latter-day prophets and Apostles. Many of them have spoken on this topic in settings where they specifically addressed the young adults of the Church. I have gathered a few of my favorite talks at the end of this chapter, and I would encourage you to read them in their entirety.

If you are committed to and striving for a celestial marriage, you will need to begin with a willingness to date. Dating can be enjoyable or an awkward mess. I remember one time in college, I was particularly down after a failed relationship attempt. In my semi-bitter state, I vowed to take time away from women. Really, this was just an overreaction to the fact that my heart was hurting. I had a wise roommate who gave me some profound counsel: "Don't hang yourself with the celibacy rope."[10] This simple yet straightforward advice helped snap me out of my funk. Remember, if you don't date, you won't find a mate.

Elder Dallin H. Oaks has given heartfelt counsel about dating. He can speak not only from experience early in life, but later in life as well since his first wife passed away and he successfully dated and remarried a second time. He taught the value of dating, as opposed to the world's approach to relationships: hanging out.

10 Questions to Answer
after Serving a Mission

Simple and more frequent dates allow both men and women to "shop around" in a way that allows extensive evaluation of the prospects. The old-fashioned date was a wonderful way to get acquainted with a member of the opposite sex. It encouraged conversation. It allowed you to see how you treat others and how you are treated in a one-on-one situation. It gave opportunities to learn how to initiate and sustain a mature relationship. None of that happens in hanging out.[11]

He went on to give counsel to both the men and the women. I feel his words, if followed, will produce many more opportunities to attract the person you are looking for and assist you in the becoming the person you are trying to be. First, to the men.

Men, if you have returned from your mission and you are still following the boy-girl patterns you were counseled to follow when you were 15, it is time for you to grow up. Gather your courage and look for someone to pair off with. Start with a variety of dates with a variety of young women, and when that phase yields a good prospect, proceed to courtship. It's marriage time. That is what the Lord intends for His young adult sons and daughters. Men have the initiative, and you men should get on with it. If you don't know what a date is, perhaps this definition will help. I heard it from my 18-year-old granddaughter. A "date" must pass the test of three p's: (1) planned ahead, (2) paid for, and (3) paired off.[12]

I love how candid Elder Oaks is in presenting the need to move forward. Basically, he is telling returned missionary men to get some guts and ask women on dates. All of the counsel you received and hopefully followed about not dating until sixteen and avoiding steading dating in high school is old news. Now it is time to adjust your dating lens to have them become more frequent and inexpensive.

Do not worry about doing marathon dates either. That is one thing I saw in high school youth all the time. Day dates consisted of multiple activities, leading up to a school dance that required a couple to be together for up to twelve hours a day. Your dates can honestly be just an hour or even a half hour long. The whole goal is to get to know one another. If you mutually want to continue getting to know each other more, the dates can certainly get more frequent and last longer.

Now, for the sisters.

Young women, resist too much hanging out, and encourage dates that are simple, inexpensive, and frequent. Don't make it easy for young men to hang out in a setting where you women provide the food. Don't subsidize freeloaders. An occasional group activity is OK, but when you see men who make hanging out their primary interaction with the opposite sex, I think you should lock the pantry and bolt the front door.

If you do this, you should also hang up a sign, "Will open for individual dates," or something like that. And, young women, please make it easier for these shy males to ask for a simple, inexpensive date. Part of making it easier is to avoid implying that a date is something very serious. If we are to persuade young men to ask for dates more frequently, we must establish a mutual expectation that to go on a date is not to imply a continuing commitment. Finally, young women, if you turn down a date, be kind. Otherwise you may crush a nervous and shy questioner and destroy him as a potential dater, and that could hurt some other sister.[13]

I remember one of my BYU professors giving the sisters counsel in our class. With a wealth of experience in the field of family science, he shared this insight: "85 percent of men will ask out a woman who has first showed interest in him."[14] This rings true for most men because we are so worried about being rejected. There are some men so worried about getting turned down that they would rather not ask someone out at all.

Sisters, this is where you can help your own cause. Sure, there will be the guys who ask you out and you are not interested. Then there will be the times when you cannot get a man to ask you out, even though you have dropped enough hints for him to win the game of *Clue*. But that is the dance we call dating. You can express interest in a man without looking or sounding desperate. And as you communicate well enough (and for long enough), most men, despite our cluelessness nature at times, will get the hint. If he is not afraid of getting rejected, then he is much more likely to ask you out.

When you have gone on enough dates that you are exclusive—boyfriend and girlfriend, or a couple—now is the time to determine if your significant other is someone you want to spend eternity with. Make sure you go on enough dates to really see the person whom you are dating. I believe in long courtships and short engagements. Make sure you see your date in as many situations as possible before you commit to marriage.

How Am I Striving to Create a Celestial Marriage?

It would be beneficial to see your significant other with his or her family. Often, how he or she treats parents and siblings can give you great insight into how he or she might treat you when you are married. Try to see them when they are spiritual, angry, sick, happy, sad, and crazy. Most of us put our best foot forward when we go on dates. We dress up, smell good, and act kind. The reality is we all are flawed and imperfect, so does the face you are seeing accurately reflect the heart that lies beneath?

This causes some men and women to fear getting married: it takes too long or can be too heartbreaking. President Monson gave comforting counsel,

> I realize there are many reasons why you may be hesitating to take that step of getting married. If you are concerned about providing financially for a wife and family, may I assure you that there is no shame in a couple having to scrimp and save. It is generally during these challenging times that you will grow closer together as you learn to sacrifice and to make difficult decisions. Perhaps you are afraid of making the wrong choice. To this I say that you need to exercise faith. Find someone with whom you can be compatible. Realize that you will not be able to anticipate every challenge which may arise, but be assured that almost anything can be worked out if you are resourceful and if you are committed to making your marriage work.[15]

Maybe you are just having too much fun dating around and enjoying the single life. All you have to worry about is yourself, and life is easier and simpler. I strongly caution you against delaying marriage for selfish reasons. My brother-in-law gets so frustrated with the Peter Pan syndrome, where young men never want to grow up. Do not run away from the greatest adventure! More happiness and joy awaits you in a celestial marriage than you could ever dream of alone. President Monson counseled,

> Perhaps you are having a little too much fun being single, taking extravagant vacations, buying expensive cars and toys, and just generally enjoying the carefree life with your friends. I've encountered groups of you running around together, and I admit that I've wondered why you aren't out with the young ladies.
>
> Brethren, there is a point at which it's time to think seriously about marriage and to seek a companion with whom you want to spend eternity. If you choose wisely and if you are committed to the success of your marriage, there is nothing in this life which will bring you greater happiness.[16]

Now, what if you successfully start dating and it led to steady dating, but after a time you realize it is not going to work? What if you are blindsided by a breakup when you think everything is going blissfully well? Whether you are the one instigating the breakup or are blindsided by the split, both are painful. There is some tremendous practical advice about relationships I gleaned as a young single adult from John Bytheway. One of my favorite quotes from his audio talk was, "The wrong one is the right one to lead you to the best one."[17]

I dated frequently while in college and enjoyed getting to know new people. I had my share of breakups where I was both the dumper and the dumpee. When I met my future bride, I had just come off a serious relationship. Her situation was the same. We became friends and strengthened that friendship for months before either one of us proceeded to serious dating. To hear her tell the story, she had to invite me over to her place to make banana bread a hundred times (serious exaggeration here; it was only about five or six times).

I share this with you to give you hope. The person who broke your heart could be the catalyst that leads you to your eternal companion. So do not get all that discouraged about breakups; you can survive them without going to pieces.[18]

The other steady dating possibility is the eventual progression to engagement and marriage. So how do you know if the person you are starry-eyed about is truly the one you should spend eternity with? Many servants of the Lord have weighed in on this critical decision. Here is some of the best wisdom that I have found. First, from President Monson,

> In making a decision as momentous as whom you will marry, I suggest you seek the help of your parents. Take the time to confide in them, for they will not leave you nor forsake you. They love you dearly and want for a precious daughter or stalwart son the best in life and the ultimate promises of eternity.[19]

Your parents have a vested interest in whom you are dating and who you will eventually marry because they love you—and you will have their grandchildren. While it is true that the marriage decision is yours alone, do not spite your parent's counsel. Ask them about their dating years and how they came to the conclusion to get married. You can learn much from their wisdom and experiences.

10 Questions to Answer
after Serving a Mission

Parents and close friends also help you see "blind spots" in a relationship. I am confident you are familiar with the blind spots that are inherent from driving. The same analogy works with relationships. We say "love is blind." A person will overemphasize the good in their significant other and willingly overlook the bad qualities. Trust the judgment of those who have your best interest at heart. Again, you will ultimately have the make the decision to spend eternity with someone, but there is valuable counsel that can come from others who see your relationship from a different angle.

Elder Holland gave counsel about how to know if someone is not the right one for you. He taught,

> In a dating and courtship relationship, I would not have you spend five minutes with someone who belittles you, who is constantly critical of you, who is cruel at your expense and may even call it humor. Life is tough enough without having the person who is supposed to love you leading the assault on your self-esteem, your sense of dignity, your confidence, and your joy. In this person's care you deserve to feel physically safe and emotionally secure.[20]

Try to find someone who will laugh at your humor without making you the butt of their jokes.

Compatibility is important in a relationship. In essence, this means, do we fit well together? There are many ways to evaluate your compatibility with someone that are worth your time and effort, but here I am going to stick with one of the most important: spirituality. Elder Hales said,

How Am I Striving to Create
a Celestial Marriage?

Measure the spiritual level of your potential future companions. First, if they are members of the Church, are they active and fully committed, or are they passive or antagonistic? Second, if they are not members, are they receptive to the gospel and its teachings, or are they noncommittal or antagonistic?

If you marry an active member in the temple for time and all eternity in the new and everlasting covenant, will you have problems? Yes. Will you be able to solve them? Yes. Will your chance be better to solve them and strengthen your testimony than if you had not married in the temple? Yes. But if you marry somebody who is antagonistic to the Church or passive toward the gospel, you are placing yourself in a position where you will find someday that you may have to choose between that individual and the Church. That is a very heavy responsibility.

When you are choosing your companion, make sure that both of you have a desire for a celestial marriage relationship, a desire to have a companion for eternity, a desire to have a family for eternity, and a desire to live in the presence of our Heavenly Father.[21]

A word to single sisters who may be wondering about not having this beautiful opportunity for love and marriage in this life. I know this worry is real and genuine for many of you. I hope a few words from Elder Oaks will help.

If you are just marking time waiting for a marriage prospect, stop waiting. You may never have the opportunity for a suitable marriage in this life, so stop waiting and start moving. Prepare yourself for life—even a single life—by education, experience, and planning. Don't wait for happiness to be thrust upon you. Seek it out in service and learning. Make a life for yourself. And trust in the Lord.[22]

I have heard Sister Sheri Dew, CEO of Deseret Book, single and sixty-one, speak on the subject. Being single in this life is not what she wanted or anticipated. Many people have asked her about being single in a church so focused on family. Her insight was priceless:

> My life has not turned out like I thought it would or hoped it would. And with every passing year, I think, "Ok, seriously? Really? We're going to click off another birthday here and I'm still not married? Really?" . . . There are certain things that because of the nature of my life I totally understand. I understand disappointment. I understand loneliness, I really get that. I understand what feels like rejection. I understand a feeling of isolation. . . .
>
> In the times of pain, I simply don't know how I would have survived if it weren't for coming to understand that when the Lord said he would heal our broken hearts, he was serious about it and that was physical and tangible and real. I don't know what I would have done if I hadn't learned a long time ago that I could find comfort solace and instruction in the temple. I don't know what I would have done if I hadn't been able to figure out what it feels like to open the scriptures and see something leap off the page. . . .
>
> When people say to me, and they do a lot, how can you be happy in a church that is so family oriented? Part of the reason is I don't actually see myself as single. I think of myself as not yet married. I've never seen myself as single; I

just don't understand why I am having to wait so long. But another part of the reason is because every part of joy in my life has come because of the gospel, not in spite of it.[23]

For those at the point of taking your relationship to the next level, how can you know for sure if he or she is "the one"? First, recognize the fallacy that there is not a "one and only" soul mate you made covenants in the premortal existence with. The *Saturday's Warrior* nonsense does not sit well with me.[24]

Instead, the delicate balance between agency and inspiration takes its course in your relationship. God has given you the ability to choose for yourself; nevertheless, He admonishes you to counsel with Him in all your doings.[25] How do you know then when you are making the choice and when God is directing you? Elder Bruce R. McConkie shared this insight about his experience choosing his wife.

> How do you choose a wife? . . . Maybe it will be a little shock to you, but never in my life did I ever ask the Lord whom I ought to marry. It never occurred to me to ask Him. I went out and found the girl I wanted; she suited me; I evaluated and weighed the proposition, and it just seemed a hundred percent to me as though this ought to be. Now, if I'd done things perfectly, I'd have done some counseling with the Lord, which I didn't do; but all I did was pray to the Lord and ask for some guidance and direction in connection with the decision I'd reached. A more perfect thing to have done would have been to counsel with Him relative to the decision and get a spiritual confirmation that the conclusion, which I by my agency and faculties had arrived at, was the right one.[26]

10 Questions to Answer after Serving a Mission

Remember that two people's agency are involved when it comes to getting married. If a guy thinks he can get a revelation and use that as leverage to make a woman marry him, he ought to be smacked on the head. Elder Oaks taught,

> I have heard of cases where a young man told a young woman she should marry him because he had received a revelation that she was to be his eternal companion. If this is a true revelation, it will be confirmed directly to the woman if she seeks to know. In the meantime, she is under no obligation to heed it. She should seek her own guidance and make up her own mind. The man can receive revelation to guide his own actions but he cannot properly receive revelation to direct hers. She is outside his stewardship.[27]

As you search for that balance of revelation and inspiration in finding a future spouse, the magnitude of this decision can't be overstated. President Kimball said, "The greatest single factor affecting what you are going to be tomorrow, your activity, your attitudes, your eventual destiny is the one decision you make that moonlit night when you ask that individual to be your companion for life. That's the most important decision of your entire life!"[28]

President Hinckley echoed that counsel on three different occasions.[29] The reason this decision is so vital is because of the long lasting impact it will have on your life, the life of your spouse, and the children you bring into your marriage. My children will have to look like me for the rest of this earth life!

Once you have made that decision, stick to it. I get so tired of hearing the trite phrase, "I fell in love." You do not fall in love like you fall out of bed. You either grow in love or you wilt in love. Please understand this powerful truth: love is a choice.[30] I love my wife because I choose to love her. To her celestial credit, she makes that easy to do most of the time. But love is not something that simply is thrust upon you or carried out without any agency on your part.

The best piece of marriage counsel I ever received was, "A happy wife is a happy life." I believe in this and have seen it in my own life. President Hinckley taught that truth this way: "I am satisfied that a happy marriage is not so much a matter of romance as it is an anxious concern for the comfort and well-being of one's companion."[31]

Stop worrying about the person you thought you married and get to work on the relationship with the person you are married to. Love is a choice and is best cultivated by giving your whole self to your spouse. Notice that there is only one person God commands you to love with all of your heart other than Him.[32] "Thou shalt love thy wife with all thy heart, and shalt cleave unto her and none else" (D&C 42:22). The word *cleave* is fascinating because it is an oxymoron in and of itself. It means to both split apart and bind together.

The best marriage advice ever given is from the Lord himself after He married Adam and Eve in the Garden of Eden, "Therefore shall a man leave his father and his mother, and shall cleave unto his wife" (Moses 3:23). Leave (or split apart) from the family you came from and bind (or stick together) with the one you have just created. There is much wisdom in leaving your parents' homes and creating your own life together—just make sure you let them visit often.

10 Questions to Answer
after Serving a Mission

Paul gave my most personally treasured counsel about marriage. "Husbands, love your wives, even as Christ also loved the church, and gave himself for it" (Ephesians 5:25). If you are loving and treating each other as the Savior loved and gave His life, certainly your marriage will be one of love and strength.

Unfortunately, we face a tidal wave of acceptance and even embracing of the plague of divorce in our society. Elder Dallin H. Oaks outlined the position of the Church on this matter. I will not go into the details here; suffice it to say, "For most marriage problems, the remedy is not divorce but repentance. Often the cause is not incompatibility but selfishness. The first step is not separation but reformation. Divorce is not an all-purpose solution, and it often creates long-term heartache."[33] Some of you have probably experienced the sting of divorce in your own family. I hope the celestial marriage you are preparing for or are already living can be one of happiness and joy, founded upon Christ. Challenges will certainly come to your marriage, but you can work them out together if you rely upon Him. President Monson said,

> If any of you are having difficulty in your marriage, I urge you to do all that you can to make whatever repairs are necessary, that you might be as happy as you were when your marriage started out. We who are married in the house of the Lord do so for time and for all eternity, and then we must put forth the necessary effort to make it so. I realize that there are situations where marriages cannot be saved, but I feel strongly that for the most part they can be and should be. Do not let your marriage get to the point where it is in jeopardy.[34]

How Am I Striving to Create a Celestial Marriage?

In conclusion, I urge you to center yourself in the doctrine of the family, as contained in the family proclamation. Immerse yourself in that divine document. I know its truths are foundational for your success in an eternal, celestial family. The principles contained within it are as beautiful as the warnings are chilling.

I have great confidence in your ability to choose the Savior, choose the right spouse, choose to love, and continue faithfully in your efforts to embrace the plan God has to exalt families. President Monson taught it best,

> Choose a companion carefully and prayerfully; and when you are married, be fiercely loyal one to another. Priceless advice comes from a small framed plaque I once saw in the home of an uncle and aunt. It read, "Choose your love; love your choice." There is great wisdom in those few words. Commitment in marriage is absolutely essential.[35]

Additional Readings

- The First Presidency, "The Family: A Proclamation to the World," *Ensign*, November 1995
- Thomas S. Monson, "Priesthood Power," *Ensign*, May 2011
- Thomas S. Monson, "Whom Shall I Marry?" *New Era*, October 2004
- Dallin H. Oaks, "The Dedication of a Lifetime," CES Devotional, May 1, 2005 (reprinted in *Ensign*, June 2006)
- Jeffrey R. Holland, "How Do I Love Thee?" BYU Devotional, February 15, 2000 (reprinted in *New Era*, October 2003)

10 Questions to Answer
after Serving a Mission

- Robert D. Hales, "Celestial Marriage: A Little Heaven on Earth," BYU Devotional, November 9, 1976 (reprinted in *Ensign*, September 2011)
- Bruce R. McConkie, "Agency or Inspiration," BYU Devotional, February 27, 1973 (reprinted in *New Era*, January 1975)
- Dallin H. Oaks, "Divorce," *Ensign*, May 2007
- Lynn G. Robbins, "Agency and Love in Marriage," *Ensign*, October 2000
- D. Todd Christofferson, "Why Marriage, Why Family," *Ensign*, May 2015
- Bonnie L. Oscarson, "Defenders of the Family Proclamation," *Ensign*, May 2015
- John Bytheway, *What I Wished I'd Known When I Was Single* (Salt Lake City: Deseret Book, 1999); free digital download from Deseret Book

Notes

1. Thomas S. Monson, "Whom Shall I Marry?" *New Era*, October 2004.
2. Those people don't ever really go away because, once you get married, they want to know when you will start having kids.
3. Thomas S. Monson, "Whom Shall I Marry?"
4. Ibid.
5. Robert D. Hales, "Celestial Marriage: A Little Heaven on Earth," BYU Devotional, November 9, 1976 (reprinted in *Ensign*, September 2011).

6. See D&C 132:7.

7. Thomas S. Monson, "Whom Shall I Marry?"

8. D&C 4:6.

9. David A. Bednar in an interview with Sheri Dew, available on www.mormonchannel.org, under the program "Conversations," episode 1. Quoted portion begins shortly after the thirty-one-minute mark.

10. Thanks to Morgan McDuffie for his simple yet profound counsel.

11. Dallin H. Oaks, "The Dedication of a Lifetime," CES Devotional, May 1, 2005 (reprinted in *Ensign*, June 2006).

12. Ibid.

13. Ibid.

14. Thank you, Dr. Brent Barlow, for your wealth of wisdom in all my family science classes.

15. Thomas S. Monson, "Priesthood Power," *Ensign*, May 2011.

16. Ibid.

17. John Bytheway, *What I Wished I'd Known When I Was Single* (Salt Lake City: Deseret Book, 1999).

18. See M. Gawain Wells, "Breaking Up Without Going to Pieces: When Dating Doesn't End in Marriage," *Ensign*, June 1982.

19. Thomas S. Monson, "Priesthood Power."

20. Jeffrey R. Holland, "How Do I Love Thee?" BYU Devotional, February 15, 2000 (reprinted in *New Era*, October 2003).

21. Robert D. Hales, "Celestial Marriage: A Little Heaven on Earth."

22. Dallin H. Oaks, "The Dedication of a Lifetime."

23. Sheri Dew in an interview with Heidi Swinton, available on www.mormonchannel.org, under the "Conversations," episode 54. The quoted portion begins just after the thirty-five-minute mark.

24. President Spencer W. Kimball once said, "'Soul mates' are fiction and an illusion; and while every young man and young woman will seek with all diligence and prayerfulness to find a mate with whom life can be most compatible and beautiful, yet it is certain that almost any good man and any good woman can have happiness and a successful marriage if both are willing to pay the price" (BYU Devotional, September 7, 1976 [reprinted in *Ensign*, October 2002].).

    Joseph Fielding Smith taught, "We have no scriptural justification, however, for the belief that we had the privilege of choosing our parents and our life companions in the spirit world. This belief has been advocated by some, and it is possible that in some instances it is true, but it would require too great a stretch of the imagination to believe it to be so in all, or even in the majority of cases. Most likely we came where those in authority decided to send us. Our agency may not have been exercised to the extent of making choice of parents and posterity" (Joseph Fielding Smith, *The Way to Perfection* [Salt Lake City: Deseret Book, 1984].).

How Am I Striving to Create a Celestial Marriage?

25. Alma 37:37.

26. Bruce R. McConkie, "Agency or Inspiration," BYU Devotional, February 27, 1973 (reprinted in *New Era*, January 1975).

27. Dallin H. Oaks, "Revelation," BYU Devotional, September 29, 1981 (reprinted in *New Era*, September 1982).

28. Spencer W. Kimball, *Teachings of Spencer W. Kimball* (Salt Lake City: Bookcraft, 1995), 301.

29. Gordon B. Hinckley, *Church News*, June 14, 1997; *Ensign*, May 1998; BYU Devotional, October 31, 2006.

30. Lynn G. Robbins, "Agency and Love in Marriage," *Ensign*, October 2000.

31. Gordon B. Hinckley, "What God Hath Joined Together," *Ensign*, May 1991.

32. Matthew O. Richardson, "Three Principles of Marriage," *Ensign*, April 2005.

33. Dallin H. Oaks, "Divorce," *Ensign*, May 2007.

34. Thomas S. Monson, "Priesthood Power," *Ensign*, May 2011.

35. Ibid.

Question 8

How Well Am I Living
the Law of Chastity?

"Much of the happiness that may come to you in this life will depend on how you use this sacred power of creation."[1]

—*President Boyd K. Packer*

I BELIEVE THIS truth taught by President Packer with all my of heart. Unfortunately, you have many voices in the world advocating exactly the opposite, such as, "Sexual freedom is liberating." Others shout, "Doing whatever you want with your body will make you happy." Do not be deceived! I hope I can adequately express to you the doctrine about chastity and some helpful counsel about how to remain committed to living it. Because this topic is so critical to your success after the mission, I will spend more time discussing it than anything else in this book.

I see the world's approach to law of chastity as one of damage control. Some people believe that teenagers and young adults are just raging hormonal beasts who are incapable of exercising any kind of control over their unrelenting passions. Therefore, we apparently should have them inflict as little sexual destruction as possible and give them contraceptives free of charge so there are not any unwanted diseases and babies.

I simply do not believe in this mentality. Instead, I choose to lookd at the doctrine of sexual purity in this way: "True doctrine, understood, changes attitudes and behavior. The study of the doctrines of the gospel will improve behavior quicker than a study of behavior will improve behavior."[2] When we understand the truth behind the divine sexual power God has given us and what His expectations are for using it, then I believe such passions can be controlled—and not just controlled but used with His approval for righteous purposes.

My favorite quote about the precious gift of chastity comes from Elder Jeffrey R. Holland, who stated, "*The only control placed on us is self-control*—self-control born of respect for the divine sacramental power this gift represents."[3]

Let us be clear when we are talking about the law of chastity. The family proclamation gives the best definition of this law I have ever found: "The sacred powers of procreation are to be employed only between man and woman, lawfully wedded as husband and wife."[4] Synonyms for *chastity* are morality or sexual purity. We also need to be clear how the scriptures define sexuality. Two frequently used words in the scriptures are *fornication* and *adultery*. *Fornication* is having sexual relations with someone outside of the bonds of marriage. *Adultery* is having sexual relations with someone other than your spouse outside the bonds of marriage. Another word frequently used in reference to chastity is *fidelity*, which is being totally loyal and faithful to your spouse in matters of sexuality.

I mentioned the need to be clear about matters of chastity because far too often in the Church there is confusion and embarrassment about this topic. This simply cannot happen.

One humorous situation was related to me by a fellow religious educator who had recently been put in the bishopric. With the responsibility of doing semi-annual interviews with the Beehives and deacons now a part of his calling, my friend proceeded to give a limited-use temple recommend to a twelve-year-old woman. He asked, "Do you live the law of chastity?" She responded in the affirmative. Wanting to be sure she understood what he was asking, my friend asked a follow-up question, "Could you explain for me in one sentence what the law of chastity is?" Her response was humorous in its innocence: "Isn't that where you are supposed to love everybody?" No . . . that would be the law of charity, not chastity.

hahaha

On a more serious note, this topic truly deserves the utmost sensitivity and care when being discussed because of its sacred nature. Unfortunately, this then leads some in the Church to not talk about matters of sexuality unless a Sunday School lesson mandates it. All this does is create awkwardness whenever the topic is approached in a gospel or family setting. Truth can dispel the embarrassment! Notice the first sentence in the *For the Strength of Youth* pamphlet in the section on sexual purity: "Physical intimacy between husband and wife is beautiful and sacred." The two words used to describe sexuality are beautiful and sacred, not, say, bad and icky.

The world so openly glamorizes and exploits this sacred power, using such debasing phrases as "sex sells," that the only

How Well Am I Living
the Law of Chastity?

thing many of the youth in the Church hear is, "No, no! Don't do that!" The message is not "no, no"; the message is "not yet." Sexual intimacy with your spouse is so good and wonderful that expressing the gift of your full self is worth the wait.

I feel there are young women in the Church who hear the message about being virtuous in the negative far too often, meaning all they hear about chastity are the don'ts and the penalties that come if this law is not kept. This can possibly lead to a "dirty" or "unclean" feeling after consummating the marriage with their husbands on their honeymoon night. That should be the furthest feeling in their minds after taking so much care to wait until their wedding day.

Another misconception I have seen about intimacy in marriage is that the only time a couple should be physically intimate is when they are trying to have a baby. This simply is not true. Procreation is a natural result of intimacy in marriage, but another reason for sex in marriage is "for the expression of love between husband in wife."[5] Sometimes there are more powerful ways to say *I love you* than through words, and physical intimacy is one of those God-given ways for doing so between husband and wife.

One of my favorite professors at BYU in the field of family science was Dr. Brent Barlow. He shared an experience with us about understanding "the spiritual and emotional damage that come from sharing sexual intimacy outside of marriage."[6] While early in his career, Dr. Barlow was teaching at a university in the eastern United States. In class one day, the topic of having an affair came up—which is not uncommon in the field of family science.

10 Questions to Answer
after Serving a Mission

Students began to share their family experiences, where either their mothers or their fathers had been unfaithful in the marriage. Some of the students even expressed the inevitability of their own probable affairs once they reached marriage. Finally, one student asked Dr. Barlow if he had ever had an affair. He answered no. Somewhat surprised, the student inquired, "Well, why not?"

Dr. Barlow then had the opportunity to walk his students through the realities of having extramarital sexual relations. He talked about the physical, mental, emotional, and social consequences of intimacy outside of marriage, including STDs, guilt, a lowered self-worth, a warped view about real love, the loss of friendships, loss of trust in the opposite sex, broken family relationships, and so forth. As the bell rang and students started filing out of his class, Dr. Barlow said he could have kicked himself because he did not get to the most important consequence of infidelity: the spiritual one; the loss of the Holy Ghost and damaging your relationship with your Heavenly Father.

I believe one of the main reasons that Satan works so incessantly to get us to misuse this sacred power is because "the Spirit of the Lord will withdraw from one who is in sexual transgression." Without the Spirit to lead and guide us, we have to do our best with a limited mortal mind. I have watched youth who are on fire with the gospel of Jesus Christ start making mistakes with the law of chastity. Pretty soon their enthusiasm wanes, and sometimes indifference or even rebellion sets in. Most often, I hear the excuse, "I have never even felt the Holy Ghost before."

When mistakes are made regarding sexual purity, the only answer is repentance. Jesus Christ's mercy is the only thing that

How Well Am I Living
the Law of Chastity?

can cleanse us from sin and help us to truly change. Christ's grace can transform and restore us. Once we are willing, we can feel our Savior's desire to make us whole. <u>True repentance is always the answer for breaking the law of chastity. Remember, the worst part about repentance is what happens if we do not do it.</u> In this case, the loss of your companionship with the Holy Ghost to lead and guide you through your young adult life.

Notice three blessings outlined in *For the Strength of Youth* that will come from remaining sexually pure: "Remaining sexually pure helps you to be *confident* and *truly happy* and improves your ability to *make good decisions* now and in the future."[8] Living the law of chastity brings confidence because you can stand, kneel, or sit in the presence of the Lord without questioning your worth. You know that you are keeping His standard of morality and you can walk tall in His presence and in the presence of those you date. True happiness comes from keeping the commandments (see Mosiah 2:41).

Once you have confidence and happiness in your life from living the law of chastity, the natural result is the ability to make good decisions that are guided by the Spirit. I recently watched Brother Brad Wilcox (LDS author and speaker) brilliantly show why true happiness comes from keeping the commandments, and especially the law of chastity. He discussed how indulging in self-stimulation, pornography, and even immodesty throughout one's life will lead to a wedding day where you have a warped view of sexuality. When you get married, intimacy is not just about what you get; it is also about what you give. When you have an appetite that is constantly indulged, all you want to do is take, and in marriage nobody wants to be the faucet to a spouse's unending drain. Selfishness and selflessness have much to do with marriage and therefore the law of chastity.

Elder Jeffrey R. Holland taught this doctrine so powerfully in general conference that I would recommend you thoroughly pour over his talk. We speak so often of the dangers of pornography because of the addiction and damage it can cause to our marriages, but Elder Holland took it one step further. He said, "If we stop chopping at the branches of this problem and strike more directly at the root of the tree, not surprisingly we find lust lurking furtively there."[9] He then went on to teach the difference between love and lust in such a profound way.

> Why is lust such a deadly sin? Well, in addition to the completely Spirit-destroying impact it has upon our souls, I think it is a sin because it defiles the highest and holiest relationship God gives us in mortality—the love that a man and a woman have for each other and the desire that couple has to bring children into a family intended to be forever. Someone said once that true love must include the idea of permanence. True love endures. But lust changes as quickly as it can turn a pornographic page or glance at yet another potential object for gratification walking by, male or female. True love we are absolutely giddy about—as I am about Sister Holland; we shout it from the housetops. But lust is characterized by shame and stealth and is almost pathologically clandestine—the later and darker the hour the better, with a double-bolted door just in case. Love makes us instinctively reach out to God and other people. Lust, on the other hand, is anything but godly and celebrates self-indulgence. Love comes with open hands and open heart; lust comes with only an open appetite.[10]

How Well Am I Living
the Law of Chastity?

Alma taught it this way to his son Shiblon: "bridle all your passions that you may be filled with love" (Alma 39:12). I also deduce that the converse is true—unbridled passion fills you with lust. I think of a two thousand pound stallion being controlled with just a four-inch bit as part of a bridle on its head. If a horse is in control, it can be useful to its master. I think the same goes for us, in that when we are in control of our desires, we can become a useful instrument in the hands of our Master.

One of my good friends taught that immorality leads to hate, not love.[11] I would like to add to his idea by saying that lust can also lead to hate instead of love. When all you want to do is possess someone for your selfish exploitation, this lust can produce disastrous consequences. The Bible provides numerous examples of this. After King David lay with Bathsheba, had her husband, Uriah, killed in battle, and took Bathsheba to wife, Nathan the prophet revealed to the king that there would be severe consequences for his actions, including that violence would always continue within David's family (see 2 Samuel 11–12).

A different story, this in 2 Samuel 13, is chilling. King David's son Amnon desired his half-sister Tamar. The word *love* is used at least four times to describe how Amnon felt about Tamar. I have my seminary students change the word *love* to *lust*. Amnon devised a cunning plan to lure her into his bedroom by feigning sickness. While providing Amnon a meal to help him get better, Tamar was then raped by her half-brother. "Then Amnon hated her exceedingly; so that the hatred wherewith he hated her was greater than the love wherewith he had loved her. And Amnon said unto her, Arise, be gone" (2 Samuel 13:15). Amnon's lust for

10 Questions to Answer after Serving a Mission

Tamar lead him to get what he wanted, and then he dismiss her as if she were simply an object. Beware of being enslaved to lust!

Keeping the law of chastity has everything to do with keeping passions in check with what God would want, and also doing all we can to establish love as the primary motive for our actions. Therefore, if pornography is still has a tractor beam pull on you, it is time to get some help. I would recommend two sources—one LDS and one not—to help curb your appetite and cultivate a palate for charity.

First, overcomingpornorgraphy.org. This brilliant resource (in connection with the Church's addiction recovery program) will walk you through the process of overcoming pornography through the Atonement. It can help, whether you are a user of pornography or if someone you love has the addiction.

Second, a non-LDS site that is doing an incredible job of teaching about the dangers of pornography to a non-religious audience. It is fightthenewdrug.org. I watched their presentation recently to the junior high students whom I teach seminary to. I was quite thoroughly impressed with their content and commitment to eradicating pornography use in the world. Much of their material will help you understand scientifically and socially the dangers pornography presents to us as individuals, families, and our societies around world.

Now, to those who understand this doctrine but simply need some help in resisting the temptation to move beyond what is appropriate in your relationships, I hope I can help. The most common question I am asked in seminary about relationships is, "Where is the line?" This is implying, "Where am I on safe ground?" and, "When do I have to talk to the bishop?"

How Well Am I Living
the Law of Chastity?

The two sentences I have found most helpful in answering these questions come from *For the Strength of Youth* and *True to the Faith*. They are, "Never do anything that could lead to sexual transgression,"[12] and more specifically, "Determine now that you will never do anything outside of marriage to arouse the powerful emotions that must be expressed only in marriage."[13] You have to know your limits! You have to know when enough is enough for you personally and, in all honesty, that will probably come sooner for you men than it will for women.

There is a clear line that we are asked not to cross, and it is outlined in *For the Strength of Youth*, "Before marriage, do not participate in passionate kissing, lie on top of another person, or touch the private, sacred parts of another person's body, with or without clothing. Do not do anything else that arouses sexual feelings. Do not arouse those emotions in your own body."[14] A few inquiries common among my seminary students include, "But what about kissing? Is kissing okay? Does kissing cross the line?"

Whenever my students come into my office at the seminary building, quite frequently they see a white pamphlet on my shelf with a huge heart on the cover that says, "Is kissing sinful?" Almost always, this is a great conversation starter. When they ask about its contents, I ask my students to answer the question on the pamphlet's cover. When they hesitate, I offer a few additional questions to help. "Is it sinful for me to kiss my wife?" No, they respond. "Is it sinful for me to kiss someone else's wife"? Yes. Then I reiterate the first question, "Is kissing sinful?" After pondering for a few more seconds, most get the right answer: "It depends." It depends on what? Not just on the kind of kiss, but, more importantly, on you! Is kissing sinful? That depends on you. What is your motive? Are you expressing genuine affection or are you doing it just to feel good?

I think many of the troubles couples run into in their relationships have to do with communication, especially physical communication. Generally speaking, a kiss means something different to a man than it does to a woman. Unfortunately, men sometimes suffer from a form of brain damage called "kiss now, think later" syndrome. A woman might be thinking, *He cares about me and wants to be with me*, whereas a man might only be thinking, *This feels really good*.

Sisters, if you are unsure about a man's motives when he is willing to kiss you, perhaps you could say "What does a kiss mean to you?" I give this counsel to you because I think some boys are willing to give love to get physical intimacy and some girls are willing to give intimacy to get love. If you are willing to put your lips on someone else's face, you better be ready to back it up with more than just your mouth. A kiss can mean so much more than just a physical gratification of your passions. A kiss can be a commitment of your heart and mind, and it can signal a willingness to back up the physical affection with mental, emotional, and spiritual too.

President Spencer W. Kimball taught, "Kissing has been prostituted and has degenerated to develop and express lust instead of affection, honor, and admiration. To kiss in casual dating is asking for trouble. What do kisses mean when given out like pretzels and robbed of sacredness?"[15] A frequent term used where I grew up amongst LDS kids was the NCMO (pronounced "nick-moe"). It stood for non-committal make out. I cannot think of too many stupider things you can do in your dating relationships than this: gratifying the physical without any willingness to engage in the other aspects of a healthy relationship. If you insist on this kind of activity, do not be too surprised if you end up pushing the boundaries of the law of chastity further than you should go.

Remember, your commitment to be chaste rests on you. Therefore, I share the parable of the sandcastle. When you go to the beach to build a sandcastle, you need to do so in semi-wet sand. As you begin to build, you can see the ocean waves lightly lapping onto the shore. Without any further delay, you start digging a large moat around the castle. This will stop the waves as the tide moves in from low to high. With the chasm dug, you continue building the fortress of your dreams.

But just as surely as you excavated the sand around your castle, the water continues to creep ever closer. Eventually, it spills over into your well-constructed moat. You cheer with your friends as you have foiled the wave's power to override your castle. Now you get to work feverishly rebuilding your moat by eliminating the water and shoring up the walls once again. You must do both. If you only drain the water, the erosion will ultimately prove too costly. This takes an unyielding commitment to protect the castle. The line carved around the castle must be reinforced over and over again.[16]

I hope you can see the parallels that can be drawn to your unyielding commitment to stay morally clean. Elder Richard G. Scott taught it this way,

Firmly establish personal standards. Choose a time of deep spiritual reflection, when there is no pressure on you, and you can confirm your decisions by sacred impressions. Decide then what you will do and what you will not do to express feelings. The Spirit will guide you. Then do not vary from those decisions no matter how right it may seem when the temptation comes. . . . The realization of your dreams depends upon your determination to never betray your standards.[17]

your goa temple marriage oct 12

What happens if you find yourself in a potentially compromising situation, whether of your own making or by accident? My wife had a bishop once who explained one thing that could help. While teaching about the law of chastity, he counseled his young adults to be careful not to spend too much time on the couch together. If they felt the situation was getting too comfortable, he said to jump up from the couch and run into the kitchen and pull out a box of these. He then displayed a box of Lucky Charms that had been doctored to say "Chastity" Charms. His instruction to the young adults was to eat a bowl and then offer a bowl to their significant other if he or she needed one too.

Good idea!!

A great scriptural example comes from Genesis 39. Here, Joseph in Egypt is confronted with a seriously compromising situation. Potiphar's wife had taken a liking to Joseph. She even asked for him to lie with her. To his credit, Joseph refused, citing his commitment to God and to Potiphar. But Potiphar's wife continued to make passes at him. Joseph not only refused her— he tried to avoid being around her. Eventually (the way I read the text) it looks like Potiphar's wife set Joseph up. He comes into the house to do his business and she ambushed him with

How Well Am I Living
the Law of Chastity?

no one else around. "Lie with me," she forcefully insisted, while holding onto Joseph's garment.

I do not know how long this encounter lasted, but Joseph, possibly seeing no other solution, "fled, and got him out" (Genesis 39:12). What a great lesson. I would interpret this to mean, if all else fails, run! I frequently see in the scriptures that righteousness will flee wickedness. If you are ever tempted to break the law of chastity, get out. Literally run, if necessary.

I remember a very poignant moment many years ago when we were discussing this Old Testament story in seminary. A young man named Brock raised his hand and said, "I have had a situation like Joseph's. Can I share it with the class?" With all my students immediately serious and in rapt attention, I invited this senior baseball star to proceed. He shared with us a time when he was with a young woman he liked on a date. Later in the evening, they were at her house watching a movie. They began expressing affection, and she whispered in his ear that they should go further than just kissing.

Knowing that he did not want to go further but not knowing how to say it, Brock simply ignored her request. A short time later, she repeated her request with specifics. At this point, Brock ended the affectionate exchange and indicated that he needed to go home. As he "got him out" of the situation, the young woman followed him and pled for him to stay. He shared with us how difficult the temptation was to stay, but he knew he did not want to compromise his standards.

The next day at school, the young woman found him and indicated that if he was not willing to go any further physically than they did the night before, she did not want to be friends anymore. Brock knew he had made the right decision the night before. At this point, he dismissed her friendship and confirmed his commitment to God. "The Spirit can help you know when you are at risk and give you the strength to remove yourself from the situation."[18]

The following counsel from the *For the Strength of Youth* pamphlet might seem a little outdated now that you are an adult, but I would caution you from thinking that way. "Avoid situations that invite increased temptation, such as late-night or overnight activities away from home or activities where there is a lack of adult supervision."[19]

I think this can best be taught through an analogy to fasting. Have you ever gone twenty or more hours in your fast, only to have the incredible smell of food make you utter, "Ahhhh." How silly would it then be to march into the kitchen, throw open the refrigerator, and say, "In a few hours, I am going to eat everything in here," with eyes bulging and mouth drooling over such succulent food. I want you to remember this bit of wisdom: "When fasting, stay out of the kitchen."

It seems quite obvious why we should steer clear of the kitchen, but liken this to the law of chastity. We are all morally fasting, so stay out of the "kitchens" that will give you an undue opportunity to compromise your standards. I hope you will make a commitment in your own life right now to never express affection in a parked car or in a bedroom. Be careful to even be in apartments alone together. When it says "adult supervision," I know you do not need to be babysat by your parents, but having responsible friends around can have a huge influence on helping you keep the law of chastity.

Even when we are doing our best to keep the law of chastity, we might slip up with our thoughts. One of my favorite quotes is, "You can't stop a bird from flying over your head, but you can stop a bird from making a nest in your hair." I grew up in the San Francisco Bay Area, and we had plenty of seagulls around my town. I despised them a lot because they would hang around the high school and when someone least expected it, a seagull would drop a bomb on his or her head or shoulder. But unless I carried a gun around and shot all the seagulls that flew over my head, there was not much I could do about it. Just like there might not be much you can do from stopping an illicit thought or inappropriate image from flashing across your mind.

But what you do next is what matters. Think of how silly it would be to see one of your friends with a bird nesting on his or her head. That is absurd! If a bird tried to make a nest in your hair, you would bat the bird away immediately. Do the same with unwanted thoughts that fly through your brain. Do not let them ricochet around and do serious damage.

Dismiss them using one of three methods. *For the Strength of Youth* says to pray (see D&C 10:5). President Boyd K. Packer said to sing a hymn. Or you could bear your testimony to yourself. All three of these methods fil your mind with light so that the darkness will dispel. Put into your brain a constant source of truth so that the evils of the adversary must abate.

There is so much that you can download onto your digital devices, all of which is available at the touch of your fingertips.

10 Questions to Answer
after Serving a Mission

I heard one religious educator suggest making a "tithe" folder on your music player so that at least 10 percent of your music is spiritual. There are plenty of spiritual music sites you can visit too; mormonchannel.org is one of my favorite! A steady diet of mental righteousness will often yield far less weeds in the cognitive furrows of the mind.

The topic of same-sex attraction deserves more discussion than the limited amount I am giving it here. Please realize that, sooner or later, you will likely have a friend or family member who struggles with same-sex attraction. This is a complex issue with great passion being displayed on both sides. You might even find yourself struggling with this issue.

Please seek out places to find knowledge that will build faith. First and foremost, pray to Heavenly Father. He is the giver of all truth and can help you with this potentially divisive issue. Second, I recommend the Church's website www.mormonsandgays.org. Here, you will read what the official position of the Church is and also find others who will show you how to have faith when faced with this subject.

If you are struggling with same-sex attraction, my counsel is please do not leave the Church. I emphatically say that there is a place for you in it! It might take some time and effort to figure out how you fit, but you do belong here, and we want you to worship the Savior with us. If you have family or friends who struggle with this, please demonstrate charity toward them. Perhaps not unconditional love, but divine love patterned after the way Christ loves us.[20] True understanding of the cross another person bears can help you remain friends, even if you do not see eye to eye on this subject.

How Well Am I Living
the Law of Chastity?

Let me also speak briefly on the topic of sexual abuse. As with same-sex attraction, you might find a family member or friend was a victim of this heinous crime. Help them understand the following:

> Victims of sexual abuse are *not guilty of sin* and *do not* need to repent. If you have been a victim of abuse, know that you are innocent and that God loves you. Talk to your parents or another trusted adult, and seek your bishop's counsel immediately. They can support you spiritually and assist you in getting the protection and help you need. *The process of healing may take time*. Trust in the Savior. He will heal you and give you peace.[21]

Remember, someone cannot take from you what you are not willing to give. I previously used a piece of gum as an object lesson for teaching about chastity in my seminary class. I taught my students that the gum symbolized their personal choice and commitment to stay morally clean. Unfortunately, I have seen the limitation of using this object lesson. Some of my students might have seen the stick of gum literally as themselves, and if they were ever sexually taken advantage of they might see themselves as worthless, or "chewed." Or if they made a mistake and broke the law of chastity, then they could not be forgiven.

As much as I took painstaking measures to discuss the power of repentance and the Savior's Atonement after presenting this object lesson, I have stopped using it—I do not want anyone to misunderstand. Christ's divine power does not simply help you or make things better. He can make you whole! That is the mighty power He wields as Savior and Redeemer. His grace transforms us into beings of light, capable of becoming like Him. In this way, your virtue or chastity essentially is you and your commitment to living God's standard. "On your wedding day the very best gift you can give your eternal companion is your very best self—clean and pure and worthy of such purity in return."[22]

In conclusion, I give you ten items to review about your commitment to be morally clean. I pass these out to my students whenever we discuss the principles of sexual purity. You will see that much of what I use is patterned after *For the Strength of Youth* and *True to the Faith*. I hope these can encourage you to set your own personal standards for living the law of chastity. If you find others have different standards, even when they are members of the Church, let them know where you stand and the decisions you have made are deeply personal to you. Do not waver in your commitment to God's sacred standard of chastity.

1. Determine now that you will never do anything outside marriage to arouse the strong emotions that should only be expressed in marriage. Know your personal limits! "*The only control placed on us is self-control.*"[23]

2. No passionate kissing (which includes French kissing, making out, or NCMOs—non-committal make outs). Make your kisses snapshots, not overexposures.

3. Do not lie with or on top of another person. *Hazards of the horizontal!*[24] Keep four feet on the floor.

If you ever tipped your chair back in Church, I am sure you heard the phrase, *keep four on the floor*. Counting you and your date, there are four legs; keep them on the floor.

4. Do not touch the private, sacred parts of another person's body, even with clothes on. Do not do anything that arouses sexual feelings.

5. Do not arouse sexual emotions in your own body (so no pornography, no R-rated or even some PG-13 movies, and no self-stimulation).

6. Avoid situations that invite temptation, such as late-night or overnight activities away from home, or activities without supervision. *Dangers of the dark!* No parked cars or empty homes, and do no go into the bedroom of a member of the opposite gender. *Perils of privacy!* "When fasting, stay out of the kitchen."

7. Do not participate in discussions or any media that arouse sexual feelings. *Modesty is a must!* Not just in dress but also in speech and action.

8. The Holy Ghost goes to bed at midnight! Join Him.

So the Holy Ghost going to bed at midnight is a principle, not a rule. My friend Eric and I missed this valuable truth as teens because we were busy arguing with his mom about the technicalities of her rule.

As I have pondered this wise counsel, I believe it teaches that isolation plus fatigue equal disaster. In other words, being alone and being tired mean being in danger. So if you are alone with a member of the opposite sex late at night, enough times you will be in grave moral danger. When you are physically fatigued, you may do things you would not normally do. Coupling this with being alone can lead to compromising your standards.

9. Commit to being sexually pure. Do not wait until an emotional moment to make the decision, as you risk succumbing to temptation in the moment. Decide before. "Right decisions are easiest to make when we make them well in advance, having ultimate objectives in mind; this saves a lot of anguish at the fork [in the road], when we're tired and sorely tempted."[25]

10. Above all, "I must protect this house!"

This final counsel stems from an idea I borrowed from a fellow religious educator. I enjoy likening this message about morality to the sporting product *Under Armour*. Their slogan is "protect this house," meaning a sports team does not want anyone from a rival squad to come to their home field and disrespect them on their own turf.

So the rally cry is "I must protect this house!" The correlation to our physical bodies is unmistakable. We will all return to God one day to make an accounting for our lives upon the earth. How we use the "house" for our spirits will largely determine the kind of resurrected body we stand with in His divine presence. Therefore, I encourage my students to practice yelling this phrase whenever anyone wants us to compromise our commitment to be chaste. It becomes an audible reminder of our inner commitment to follow this law of chastity.

My returned missionary friend, I encourage you to continue studying this sacred topic with the additional resources listed at the end of the chapter. When you have chosen to love the man or woman of your dreams and are now engaged, there can come

↓ for sure!!

increased temptation to express physical affection too soon. Be wise in establishing physical relationship standards together as a couple.

As you continue preparing for the immediate and eternal future, I would counsel you to be prepared for your first night of intimacy together as husband and wife. My favorite resource recommended to me upon engagement was *The Act of Marriage* by Tim and Beverly LaHaye. They are a Christian couple who do a wonderful job of preparing engaged couples for their first sexual experience together. Their book is tastefully done, and they write from a Christian perspective.

I would caution you to read it separately before you are married, and read then it together after you are married. There are also many great LDS resources that help prepare you to enjoy the expression of sexual intimacy throughout your marriage. May the Lord bless you to love and live His beautifully sanctioned law of chastity.

Additional Readings

- Jeffrey R. Holland, "Of Souls, Symbols, and Sacraments," BYU Devotional, January 12, 1988
- Jeffrey R. Holland, "Place No More for the Enemy of My Soul," *Ensign*, May 2010
- David A. Bednar, "We Believe in Being Chaste," *Ensign*, May 2013
- David A. Bednar, "Ye Are the Temple of God," Ricks College Devotional, January 11, 2000 (reprinted in *Ensign*, September 2001)

- Brent A. Barlow, "They Twain Shall Be One: Thoughts on Intimacy in Marriage," *Ensign*, September 1986
- *True to the Faith*, "Chastity" and "Birth Control"
- *For the Strength of Youth*, "Sexual Purity"
- Tim and Beverly LaHaye, *The Act of Marriage: The Beauty of Sexual Love* (Grand Rapids, Michigan: Zondervan, 1976); recommended reading after you are engaged
- www.fightthenewdrug.org
- www.overcomingpornography.org

Notes

1. "Why Stay Morally Clean," *Ensign*, July 1972.
2. Boyd K. Packer, "Little Children," *Ensign*, November 1986.
3. Jeffrey R. Holland, "Personal Purity," *Ensign*, November 1998.
4. The First Presidency, "The Family: A Proclamation to the World," *Ensign*, November 1995.
5. *For the Strength of Youth: Fulfilling Our Duty to God* (Salt Lake City: Intellectual Reserve, 2012).
6. Ibid.
7. Ibid.; emphasis added.
8. Ibid.
9. Jeffrey R. Holland, "Place No More for the Enemy of My Soul," *Ensign*, May 2010.
10. Ibid.
11. John Hilton, *I Lost My Phone Number, Can I Have Yours?* (Salt Lake City: Deseret Book, 2006).

How Well Am I Living the Law of Chastity?

12. *For the Strength of Youth.*
13. *True to the Faith: A Gospel Reference* (Salt Lake City: Intellectual Reserve, 2004).
14. *For the Strength of Youth.*
15. Spencer W. Kimball, *Teachings of Spencer W. Kimball* (Salt Lake City: Bookcraft, 1995), 281.
16. Many thanks to my good friend Bill Jeffs for sharing this idea with me.
17. Richard G. Scott, BYU Devotional, March 3, 1996.
18. *For the Strength of Youth.*
19. Ibid.
20. See Russell M. Nelson, "Divine Love," *Ensign*, February 2003.
21. *For the Strength of Youth*; emphasis added.
22. Jeffrey R. Holland, "Personal Purity."
23. Ibid.
24. The four italicized phrases come from former Young Women's General President Sister Susan W. Tanner in a BYU–Idaho Devotional, November 18, 2003 (or in *New Era*, October 2004).
25. Spencer W. Kimball, "Decisions: Why It's Important to Make Some Now," *New Era*, April 1971.

Question 9

How Will I Fully Embrace the Doctrine of Conversion?

"Wouldn't this be a good time for a little self-evaluation to determine if we still have the same relationship with our Father in Heaven that we enjoyed in the mission field?"[1]

—*Elder L. Tom Perry*

I LOVE HEARING conversion stories. I am inspired and uplifted in my own resolution to follow Christ after hearing them. I know you saw "the experience of conversion"[2] with many people who chose to embrace the Savior and His restored gospel while you were a missionary. I also know that you understand the key role of the Holy Ghost in men and women experiencing conversion. What I hope to do in this chapter is taken from *Preach My Gospel*, which states, "Strive to understand the doctrine of conversion."[3] Because you have seen this process happen with your converts, now I want to deepen your understanding of this doctrine. I hope it will prove instructive for your own life so that your own personal conversion to Christ will not fail, thus leading you down the "forbidden paths" of apathy, sin, or rebellion (1 Nephi 8:28).

How Will I Fully Embrace the Doctrine of Conversion?

One thing that I have consistently noticed about lasting conversion is the need for our heart and actions to be in the same place. This principle was powerfully impressed upon me the last time I taught Jesus's famous Sermon on the Mount in Matthew 5–7. One of the main messages I get in Matthew 5 is Christ inviting us to live better lives by following Him. The old way of doing things is not going to cut it anymore. Christ raises the bar in an effort to transform our outward religious observance into actions consistent with His.

Then in Matthew 6, the Savior gives multiple examples of those whose outward religious observance is cankered by the worry of public approval. He consistently teaches that those who give alms, pray, and fast should do so in secret so that God can reward them openly. One of the best one liners is verse 21, where Christ taught, "For where your treasure is, there will your heart be also." Whatever you value most will have the controlling interest of your heart.

Finally, in Matthew 7, Christ gives us some excellent ways for us to make righteous judgments. While doing so, He cautions against the hypocrisy of noticing minor mistakes in others while there is glaring malignant sin within ourselves. We need to allow other people a chance to live the gospel and repent of their mistakes even if we are on higher spiritual ground then they are. In summary, do the right thing (Matthew 5) for the right reason (Matthew 6) and allow others the mercy to do the same (Matthew 7).

True conversion then demands that our hearts and actions are unified. You can do the right thing and still have it damn you if it was for the wrong reason. Look no further than Laman and Lemuel, who consistently obeyed but did so grudgingly, slothfully, and even resentfully. Unwilling obedience does not yield the same blessings as faithful obedience. Praying, reading scriptures, going to church, and giving service because you have to can only take you so far. There will come a point where Christ will demand all of you, not just your hands and feet.

Elder Hallstrom did a beautiful job capturing this doctrine of conversion. He taught the difference between being active in the gospel and being active in the Church.

> Some have come to think of activity in the Church as the ultimate goal. Therein lies a danger. It is possible to be active in the Church and less active in the gospel. Let me stress: activity in the Church is a highly desirable goal; however, it is insufficient. Activity in the Church is an outward indication of our spiritual desire. If we attend our meetings, hold and fulfill Church responsibilities, and serve others, it is publicly observed.
>
> By contrast, the things of the gospel are usually less visible and more difficult to measure, but they are of greater eternal importance. For example, how much faith do we really have? How repentant are we? How meaningful are the ordinances in our lives? How focused are we on our covenants?
>
> I repeat: we need the gospel *and* the Church. In fact, the purpose of the Church is to help us live the gospel. We often wonder: How can someone be fully active in the Church as a youth and then not be when they are older? How can an adult who has regularly attended and served stop coming? How can a person who was disappointed by a leader or another member allow that to end their Church participation? Perhaps the reason is they were not sufficiently converted to the gospel— the things of eternity.[4]

How Will I Fully Embrace the Doctrine of Conversion?

If your mission has had a true converting effect in your life, then it should produce not just continued activity in the Church, but also true commitment to the Savior. You should not have to keep looking over your shoulder in church, wondering who is watching what you do, be it the bishop or your parents. When you volunteer to help clean the church building, serve at the bishop's storehouse, or substitute in a Primary class, it should come from an internal desire to do right in the sight of God.

Your actions then become a natural extension of the love you have for the Savior and the sacrifice He made for you. "If ye love me, keep my commandments" (John 14:15) is about loyalty to the promise you made Christ because He is willing to offer His perfection to you. Elder Bednar taught, "The essence of the gospel of Jesus Christ entails a fundamental and permanent change in our very nature made possible through the Savior's Atonement. True conversion brings a change in one's beliefs, heart, and life to accept and conform to the will of God (see Acts 3:19; 3 Nephi 9:20) and includes a conscious commitment to become a disciple of Christ."[5]

My favorite example of conversion in the scriptures is the people of Ammon, originally known as the Anti-Nephi-Lehis. I enjoy reading about them because they demonstrate the real fruit of missionary work. We can get so caught up in the missionary adventures of Ammon and the sons of Mosiah and fail to see the real "and it came to pass" that happened with those they taught long after their missions were over.

Mormon provides a clear contrast in the Book of Mormon to the Anti-Nephi-Lehis' conversion. This foil is presented in the Amlicites. This was a group of apostate Nephites who rose up in rebellion against their brothers and joined with the Lamanites to destroy them. Alma 2 provides a glimpse of this epic battle that almost compares with something out of a Tolkien novel. Even more interesting to me is the time Mormon takes to make a prophetic commentary of this battle in Alma 3.

In three different verses,[6] Mormon uses the word *distinguished* while telling this story about the Amlicites. I do not think I fully understood the meaning of *distinguished* because I have always associated it with academics. The 1828 Webster's Dictionary defines *distinguished* as "separated or known by a mark of difference, or by different qualities."[7] This is a perfect description of what the Amlicites did. They marked themselves with red in their foreheads and called themselves Amlicites because they did not want to look like or have the same name as the Nephites. Liken with me for a minute. Are there times where we do not want to be too closely associated with being a "Molly Mormon" or "Peter Priesthood"? Maybe we do not want to be known as "one of those" returned missionaries. So we deliberately do things with our names and appearances to make sure we are distinguished from others in the Church.

> It is interesting to me that these trends of the world frequently promote a false individuality that is nothing more than a superficial and curious outward conformity. True individuality is the product of spirituality and is not a function of trinkets or ornaments attached to or hanging from parts of our body. The spiritual basis of individuality is never more evident to me than when I worship in the house of the Lord and everyone is dressed in similar white clothing, looking essentially the same. In that setting, no fads or fashion statements are necessary. The

How Will I Fully Embrace the Doctrine of Conversion?

unity and outward sameness of appearance in the temple permits the individual spirit to shine through. That, brothers and sisters, is the only type of individuality that really matters.[8]

The contrast of the Amlicites are the Anti-Nephi-Lehis. As Mormon describes them, he again uses the word *distinguished* multiple times.[9] Once they were converted and had their lives threatened by the Lamanites, Ammon brought his new members of the Church back to Zarahemla. They wanted to change their name like the Amlicites did, except this time they did not want to be known as bloodthirsty Lamanites. So they mirrored their conversion with the names of the first two faithful prophets in the Book of Mormon, Nephi and Lehi. Not only were they now distinguished in name; they also became distinguished in their actions. "They were also distinguished for their zeal towards God. . . . They were perfectly honest and upright in all things; and they were firm in the faith of Christ, even unto the end" (Alma 26:27). The most beautiful compliment Mormon pays to this great group is when he notes that they "were converted unto the Lord" and "never did fall away" (Alma 23:6).

The most important question I could give you from this contrast of conversions is: Do you want to be distinguished for your discipleship or distinguished for your dissention? How will you be remembered? Has your missionary experience ingrained the restored gospel so deeply in your bones that your family will be able to say the same thing about you that Mormon did about the people of Ammon? If you ever need to take the spiritual pulse of your post-mission life, just read Alma 5. Alma's searing questions can cut through any excuses for why we are not believing and living our testimonies.

10 Questions to Answer
after Serving a Mission

Elder Bednar described this connection between testimony and conversion. "A testimony is spiritual knowledge of truth obtained by the power of the Holy Ghost. Continuing conversion is constant devotion to the revealed truth we have received—with a heart that is willing and for righteous reasons. Knowing that the gospel is true is the essence of a testimony. Consistently being true to the gospel is the essence of conversion. We should know the gospel is true and be true to the gospel."[10]

Since "conversion is a process, not an event,"[11] we must make our conversion to Christ the quest of our spiritual journey here on earth. "Conversion takes place as we are diligent."[12] Being diligent means we are consistent. It means doing the things day after day that will ultimately transform our minds, hearts, and actions to be more Christlike. In this way, we will be comfortable in the presence of the Father and His Only Begotten Son because we have become like Them. We will become sanctified through the grace and mercy of Jesus Christ. "Although conversion is miraculous and life changing, it is a quiet miracle."[13]

Examples abound, not only in scriptures, of those whose conversion led to a consecrated life following Christ; a number of these great stories are in our own Church. Caleb Baldwin is one of those men. I hope to inspire you with the conversion story of a lesser-known Saint. Caleb's story provides evidence of one who was willing to give his life in the service of the Savior and His gospel, as well as firmly defend Joseph Smith.[14]

Caleb Baldwin was born in upstate New York on September 2, 1791. After serving in the War of 1812, Caleb married Nancy Kingsbury and moved to Ohio, where he enjoyed a life of public service. While living in Warrensville, Ohio, the Baldwins heard the Mormon missionaries preach the gospel while on their way to the Lamanites.[15] They were particularly impressed with the testimony of a recent convert, John Murdock, and requested to join the Church. In November 1830, the Baldwins were baptized by Parley P. Pratt and confirmed by Oliver Cowdery. Caleb, at age thirty-nine, joined Brother Murdock in preaching the gospel and strengthening the small branch in Warrensville. Caleb would baptize and John would confirm.

The Baldwins moved to Independence, Missouri, in the spring of 1831. Tensions with the Missourians placed Caleb in the center of one of the conflicts between the Saints and their hostile neighbors. During the battle above the Blue River, Caleb was captured and ruthlessly whipped with hickory sticks by the Missouri mobbers. He bore those scars for the rest of his life.

In 1835, Caleb joined company with Levi Jackman to preach the gospel on the way to Ohio to help build the Kirtland Temple. The had little success until arriving in Edgar County, Illinois, where they were able to baptize many, heal a woman, and even prophesy a warning about an antagonistic minister who continued to oppose their missionary work. That prophecy was later fulfilled. They eventually arrived in Kirtland in July 1835 and offered their labor on the temple. Levi Jackman said this of his missionary companion, Caleb Baldwin, "He has shone himself appointed as a preacher of the gospel on all accatins [occasions]. He is a worthy brother."[16]

After working on the Kirtland Temple, Caleb headed back to Missouri in January 1836 with a new missionary companion, Jacob Gates. On the way to Missiouri, they stopped to strengthened the Church branch Caleb had helped established in Edgar County, Illinois, for the next eight months. Their success was abundant as they rebuked evil spirits, healed the sick, spoke in tongues, and even sang well enough that three people requested baptism after hearing Caleb sing! After rejoining his family in Missiouri, the Baldwins later settled in Far West.

Caleb Baldwin's path would forever be intertwined with the Prophet Joseph Smith because of the hostilities of the Mormon war with their Missouri neighbors in 1838. Caleb was "arrested and charged with 'crimes of high treason,' including 'murder, burglary, arson, robbery, and larceny.'"[17] While pleading for a fair trial before Judge Austin A. King, the judge indicated Caleb would get a fair trial if he would renounce his religion and forsake Joseph Smith. While chained together with the Prophet, Caleb refused. With the judge finding probable cause for treason, Caleb, Joseph, and four others were the taken to Clay County and the infamous Liberty Jail await their court appearance.

The trials in the jail are well documented. Four and a half months of frozen winter misery. Caleb only received one visit from his wife shortly before Christmas. He then endured the next three brutal months with no known contact from his family, not even letters. The prisoners tried to escape twice, in early February and in early March, and both times were foiled in their attempts. A short time later, an auger handle was found in the lower level of the prison. Samuel Tillery, the jailer, was set on chaining the prisoners to the floor to prevent any further escape attempts.

I can only imagine the rage that built up in Caleb Baldwin at this point because he arose from the floor, looked the jailer in the eyes, and said, "Tillery, if you put those chains on me, I will kill you, so help me God!"[18] The jailer relented and the prisoners' hands remained free. This is significant because a short time later, Alexander McRae and Caleb Baldwin would help pen the letter from Joseph Smith to the suffering Saints, a portion of which would later be canonized as Doctrine and Covenants 121–23.

Caleb Baldwin would continue serving faithfully in Nauvoo. At one meeting, Joseph gave a sermon while standing on a barrel so all could see him. During his preaching, the Prophet lost his balance. Caleb's quick response saved Joseph from falling as he stepped in front of Joseph and allowed the Prophet to hold his shoulder for the remainder of the sermon. After the Martyrdom, Caleb and Nancy moved west with the Saints to Utah. They received their endowments and sealing in the Nauvoo Temple before leaving the city. While traveling west in a company headed by Heber C. Kimball, he was affectionately referred to as Father Baldwin. Not long after arriving in the Salt Lake Valley, Caleb Baldwin died on June 11, 1849, at fifty-seven. Brigham Young even noted Caleb's passing in his personal diary.

Caleb Baldwin's story is a source of great personal inspiration to me. The record of his life has to be constructed from the accounts of others because he left no known personal writings. Outside a few prominent events, Caleb's life largely goes unnoticed by members of the Church. But I am inspired with Caleb's conversion because he is my great-great-great-grandfather. I did not even know we were related until my grandfather, Ivan White, passed away, and I happened to look at his family tree. I even visited Liberty Jail about four months before my grandfather's death, not realizing Caleb was one of my ancestors.

From the restoration of the Church in 1830 until less than two years after the arrival of the saints in Salt Lake in 1849,

10 Questions to Answer
after Serving a Mission

Caleb Baldwin served missions, built temples, fought in Missouri, stood chained to a prophet, and raised a righteous family with his eternal wife. I hope the depth of my conversion to the Savior's gospel will leave such a priceless and inspiriting legacy for those who come after me as well. My invitation to you is to find a pioneer ancestor to be inspired by. Many lesser-known stories can be just as motivating for you personally. If you are a convert to the Church without pioneer forbearers, become the pioneer story for your descendants. They will see your example of conversion and one day rise up to call your name blessed.

If you find yourself slipping in your commitment to remain converted to Christ, remember that heart and actions must be united to give a complete offering to Him. If your heart is still in the right place, prove it with action. If your actions have become hollow, "hunger and thirst after righteousness" and you "shall be filled with the Holy Ghost" (3 Nephi 12:6).

You made consecrated covenants with God in the temple. Continue to give Him your all and He will reward you with His all. And for a Father who has "all things" (D&C 88:41), what is not included for you as His son or daughter and righteous heir?

Additional Readings

- Alma 2–3; 5; 17–25
- Matthew 5–7
- Donald L. Hallstrom, "Converted to His Gospel Through His Church," *Ensign*, May 2012
- David A. Bednar, "Converted unto the Lord," *Ensign*, November 2012
- Bonnie Parkin, "Be Ye Converted," *Ensign*, November 2013

How Will I Fully Embrace the Doctrine of Conversion?

Notes

1. L. Tom Perry, "The Returned Missionary," *Ensign*, May 2001.

2. *Preach My Gospel*, "How do I Recognize and Understand the Spirit?" (Salt Lake City: Intellectual Reserve, 2004).

3. Ibid.

4. Donald L. Hallstrom, "Converted to His Gospel Through His Church," *Ensign*, May 2012.

5. David A. Bednar, "Converted unto the Lord," *Ensign*, November 2012.

6. Alma 2:11; 3:4, 8.

7. See http://1828.mshaffer.com/d/word/distinguished.

8. David A. Bednar, "Ye Are the Temple of God," Ricks College Devotional, January 11, 2000 (reprinted in *Ensign*, September 2001).

9. Alma 23:16; 27:26–27.

10. David A. Bednar, "Converted unto the Lord."

11. *True to the Faith*, "Conversion."

12. Bonnie L. Oscarson, "Be Ye Converted," *Ensign*, November 2013.

13. *True to the Faith*, "Conversion."

14. Much of the information used for Caleb Baldwin's life events was taken from Justin Bray's article "Caleb Baldwin: Prison Companion to Joseph Smith," *Mormon Historical Studies*, Vol. 11:2, 73–91. Justin and I are both descendants.

15. See Doctrines and Covenants 32.

16. Caleb Bray, "Caleb Baldwin: Prison Companion," 73.

17. Ibid., 82.

18. Ibid., 85.

Question 10

How Will I Endure to the End through the Grace of Jesus Christ?

"I want to promise you there are great blessings in store for you if you continue to press forward with the zeal you once possessed as a full-time missionary."[1]

—Elder L. Tom Perry

I RAN TRACK and field in high school. I was not fast and I did not jump too high, but I liked the association with my fellow athletes, and I embraced the rigors of training hard. This affinity for track spilled over into a love for the Olympics. I have watched them with rapt attention over the years as I enjoy seeing feats of great power and precision on display. The stories behind the athletes are as compelling as the events are thrilling. I still remember some of the great triumphs and tragedies of different games. I still get emotional as an American athlete is awarded a gold medal with "The Star Spangled Banner" playing in the background. I guess my eyes are known to sweat sometimes.

One of the stories that stayed with me is not one of athletic triumph. In fact, it is a story of brutal heartache. Derek Redmond was a runner from England in the 1992 Olympics in Barcelona,

How Will I Endure to the End through the Grace of Jesus Christ?

Spain. He looked to be the favorite to win the four hundred meter race after posting the fastest time in qualifying and winning his previous heat. He had triumphed in sprinting opportunities before the Olympics, but had also been dogged with multiple injuries that cost him a shot at a medal during the 1988 Olympics. During his semi-final heat, tragedy struck again.

While running the race, Redmond flew out of the blocks and looked good until he approached the final turn. With half of the race to go, he tore the hamstring muscle in his right leg. He came to an awkward sputtering halt and was barely able to walk. The sadness of the moment tugs at the heart. Determined to finish the race—if only to say he completed it—he began hopping toward the finish line. After hopping the entire turn of a hundred meters, suddenly a figure came jogging onto the track. Derek's father was by his side and put an arm around his son. Derek tried to brush him off until he realized it was his father. Overcome by the emotion and knowing his Olympics dreams were shattered, he collapsed onto his father in physical and emotional anguish. With an arm around his father's shoulder, tears freely falling on his face, father and son walked together to the end of the race. The sixty-five thousand spectators rose up and applauded as a dad helped his son cross the finish line.

I still have a vivid picture of this scene mind. The beauty and symbolism that can be drawn from this story is unmistakable. All of us get hurt in life. Heartache so often strikes at the most inopportune times. Dreams come crashing down when we are unable to achieve the goals we long to accomplish. Yet, we have a Father who loves us and will help us complete any race we are determined to finish. What an example of enduring to the end.

10 Questions to Answer
after Serving a Mission

Just the word *endurance* should help you realize that life has plenty of tragedy and triumph awaiting. To endure evokes images of struggle, and yet it is persistence in the face of failure that truly makes us great in the sight of others and, most important, in the sight of our God. Endurance to me means finishing the race God has put before us, even if it means limping. As a returned missionary, you have accomplished one of the great feats in your young life, but you are only at the beginning of whole life.

Think of it this way. When a home is being built, they start with the footings and pour the concrete to set a foundation for the future structure. What you have done now is just the footings to the home of the rest of your life. You have not arrived! There is a lot to build. Joseph Smith did so much to restore the gospel to the earth, but even he only got it started. Multiple times in the Doctrine and Covenants, it says that Joseph had "power to lay the foundation of this church."[2] With your testimony cemented in the "rock of our redeemer" (Helaman 5:12), let your conversion unfold in the journey of your life.

I have continued to enjoy running since my non-glory days of high school. I stay active to try and keep my heart and spirit healthy. On occasion, I have trained for races, including simple 5Ks, medium 10Ks, difficult half-marathons, and the epicly difficult full marathon. Certainly, there are even more arduous races like Iron Mans and Ultra-Marathons, but for simplicity's sake, I want to share a sacred experience I had running my one and only marathon so far. I was on a strict training schedule with some good friends to run a marathon in Utah Valley. As I stuck to the regimen of running, I began to notice the toll it was taking on my knees. As I battled through the soreness and pain, I was determined to run this race. Though it was late May, the weather did not cooperate and snow was lightly falling the morning of the marathon. I began the race with my training buddy, but after mud-caked trails and pain in my knees slowed my pace, I found myself running alone. The problem with running alone in a race where you hurt is the nagging self-doubt that begins to pervade your thinking. After trudging to the midpoint of the race, I was muddy, soaked, and discouraged.

At this critical point in the race, I had finally caught up to my friends. I quickly changed into some dry clothes and got some food to buoy me up. Though my rest invigorated me and I wanted to continue on, as everyone set out to run again, I found myself in too much pain to continue. In defeat, I hung my head and accepted a ride home from another friend who had come to cheer everyone on at the halfway point. For the better part of the ride home, I sat slumped in my seat, dejected by my failure to finish after months of training. As I neared my home, I finally snapped my head up and had light break through to my mind. Why not finish the race at the gym? Sure, there would be no one to cheer at the finish line or help along the way, but at least I could complete what I started.

With fresh courage, I quickly got what I needed at home and headed to the gym to complete the rest of my thirteen miles. My friends, that is a long run on a stationary object. But I was undeterred in my desire to complete what I started. After a few miles of pounding on the treadmill, the pain returned, but I was able to manage it for most of the run. The last few miles were the most difficult, but I had to finish. That was the only thing pushing me forward. When I finally completed my run, I was exhausted but ecstatic. I remember returning home and emotionally shedding tears that I had completed my journey. I do not want to be overly dramatic, but this was an intense spiritual experience for me. The joy of completion far outweighed the pain it took to get there. Opposition was strong, but strength from a divine source enabled me to persist.

To truly endure and complete this race called life, we have to tap into a source far greater than ourselves. The Atonement of Jesus Christ offers us the perfect power, and it is called grace. As I have come to understand more about this doctrine, it has had a liberating effect on my discipleship. As Latter-day Saints, I think we overlook or simply misunderstand this powerful part of the Savior's Atonement. Grace is not just the help you get "after all you can do." Grace is the before, during, *and* after all you can do.

The reason you have the desire to follow Christ is His grace provides the motivation. When you move forward and act on your desire, grace is the strength you get to continue putting one foot in front of the other. Ultimately because we will fall so woefully short of the throne of God, we still need our Savior's grace to redeem our sinful souls. Grace is needed in all areas of our lives, past, present, and future, if we hope to accomplish anything of our own free will. This is why it is often defined as both a "divine" and an "enabling power."[3] We desperately need grace!

Recently, a few gifted LDS authors[4] have written about the doctrine of grace and unlocking its power in our lives. I recommend their writings in the suggested readings at the end of the chapter. I add my witness to theirs. As Latter-day Saints, I feel we sometimes get stuck on the last phrase of 2 Nephi 25:23, "after all I can do," somehow thinking we can earn salvation by doing "our best" or doing all we can. Your works demonstrate your *love* for Christ; they will never *earn* you salvation. Christ is the only perfect person to walk the face of this earth; therefore He could satisfy the demands of justice (the law). Christ then extends to us mercy. Your job is not to "get perfect," because Christ already did that. Your invitation is to come unto Christ and be perfected *in Him*. He shares His perfection with us. We become one with Him when we enter into the covenant. Our following Christ and keeping our covenants and obeying the commandments can *qualify* us for eternal life, but they will never earn it. Understanding this distinction can not only increase our reliance upon the Savior, but also help free us from the burden of trying to "perfect" ourselves, and the unnecessary guilt that accompanies this impossible task.

I love listening to the beautiful Christian anthem "Amazing Grace." The melody of the music mixed with the power of the lyrics (easily found online) can have a stirring effect on the soul. Look at the connection between the doctrine of grace and the doctrine of enduring to the end.

Study and embrace the doctrine of grace. The power that is unlocked from understanding this truth can free your mind and heart from unneeded guilt and baggage as you endure through life.

President Uchtdorf has added his apostolic witness to the doctrine of grace. He teaches the importance of merging the gift of grace with faithful obedience to God's commandments.

If grace is a gift of God, why then is obedience to God's commandments so important? Why bother with God's commandments—or repentance, for that matter? Why not just admit we're sinful and let God save us? . . . Our obedience to God's commandments comes as a natural outgrowth of our endless love and gratitude for the goodness of God. . . . <u>Grace is a gift of God, and our desire to be obedient to each of God's commandments is the reaching out of our mortal hand to receive this sacred gift from our Heavenly Father.</u>[5]

One of the more profound teaching moments about the doctrine of grace and endurance that has happened to me occurred while I was a teacher at the MTC after my mission. While reading 2 Nephi 9 as a district, a missionary paused after reading verse 18 and asked a heartfelt question: "Brother White, what does it mean to endure the crosses of the world?" Unsure of how to respond, I asked the rest of the district to share what they thought this passage could mean. But in a moment of divine clarity, understanding poured into my mind. Though this all made sense immediately in the moment, it takes a bit longer to explain in words.

Disciples of God who "take up [their] cross" (Matthew 16:24) do not find the road ends at Calvary; instead, the path is a lifelong journey. Therefore, Jesus counseled, "For which of you, intending to build a tower, sitteth not down first, and counteth the cost, *whether he have sufficient to finish it?*" (Luke 14:28; italics added). To take up the cross is not a part-time job. It requires enduring whatever God-given or worldly-imposed trials come. Nephi said, "Unless a man shall endure to the end, in following the example of the Son of the living God, he cannot be saved" (2 Nephi 31:16). Salvation through Christ demands His disciples endure as He did. This is what it took for Jesus to endure the last hours of His life, with an emphasis on the physical.

Jesus' suffering was so intense in the garden of Gethsemane that, as God, He trembled because of the pain and bled from every pore[6] for three to four hours.[7] After the betrayal at the hands of Judas,[8] Jesus was marched around to illegal trials throughout the night without sleep; first to Annas, then to Caiphais, next to Pilate, onto Herod, and finally back to Pilate[9]—all the while being mocked, smitten, and spit upon.[10] In the hopes of having Him released, Pilate first had Jesus scourged. The scourging alone could have killed Jesus if He did not have power over death.[11] One author explained it this way:

> Roman floggings were known to be terribly brutal. They usually consisted of thirty-nine lashes but frequently were a lot more than that. . . .
>
> The soldier would use a whip of braided leather thongs with metal balls woven into them. When the whip would strike the flesh, these balls would cause deep bruises or contusions, which would break open with further blows. And the whip had pieces of sharp bone as well, which would cut the flesh severely.
>
> The back would be so shredded that part of the spine was sometimes exposed by the deep, deep cuts. The whipping would have gone all the way from the shoulders down to the back, the buttocks, and the back of the legs. . . .
>
> One physician who has studied Roman beatings said, "As the flogging continued, the lacerations would tear into the underlying skeletal muscles and produce quivering ribbons of bleeding flesh." A third-century historian by the name of Eusebius described a flogging by saying, "The sufferer's veins were laid bare, and the very muscles, sinews, and bowels of the victim were open to exposure."[12]

After a crown of thorns pierced His brow, Jesus was coerced to put a massive wooden beam across a back that was nearly skinless, because of the whippings, and carry it to Golgotha. It is no wonder that, under the cumulative load of the Atonement, the soldiers compelled Simon, a Cyrenean, to carry Christ's cross.

But even as the burden became unbearable, our Savior did not falter. He finished the arduous ascent to Golgotha and endured the excruciating agony of being crucified, including having nails driven into his hands, wrists, and feet. To add to the misery, all of Jesus' pains and agonies from the Garden of Gethsemane recurred while He hung on the cross.[13] *I didn't know that*

The whole point of Jesus drinking the bitter cup is that if He did not endure to the end, then humanity would have no hope of eternal life, no ecstasy in exaltation. All would "become devils, angels to a devil, to be shut out from the presence of . . . God" (2 Nephi 9:9). Just as Jesus did not give up, neither can His disciples. *that means you!!* No load is so heavy, no burden so unbearable, compared to making an infinite payment for the sins of the world. "To endure the cross is not a tragedy; it is the suffering which is the fruit of an exclusive allegiance to Jesus Christ."[14]

My young friends, you will most certainly be called upon to endure hardship. But "if various trials are allotted to you, partake of life's bitter cups, but without becoming bitter."[15] Many of our Christian friends see an acronym in the word *grace* that will help you remember its power as you endure faithfully. *Grace* stands for **G**od's **R**iches **A**t **C**hrist's **E**xpense.[16] Truly, we are rich because God allowed His Only Begotten to suffer.

We do not have to see enduring as a plague, inflicted upon us by a vengeful god. President Uchtdorf taught,

> Enduring to the end is not just a matter of passively tolerating life's difficult circumstances or "hanging in there." Ours

How Will I Endure to the End through the Grace of Jesus Christ?

is an active religion, helping God's children along the strait and narrow path to develop their full potential during this life and return to Him one day. Viewed from this perspective, enduring to the end is exalting and glorious, not grim and gloomy. This is a joyful religion, one of hope, strength, and deliverance. . . .

By doing our best to endure to the end, a beautiful refinement will come into our lives. We will learn to "do good to them that hate [us], and pray for them which despitefully use [us]" (Matthew 5:44). The blessings that come to us from enduring to the end in this life are real and very significant, and for the life to come they are beyond our comprehension.[17]

I believe too many people in the Church think they are not going to make it to the celestial kingdom. If you were to have your gospel doctrine class close their eyes and raise their hands on which kingdom of glory they believe they will inherit, my belief is there would be far too few who have the hope that they can inherit celestial glory. They might even cite Matthew 5:48 and the impossibility of perfection as the obstacle.

Of course you are not perfect and will never be on your own. No amount of good will ever earn you a place next to the Savior. He was perfect, so you do not have to be. Through your covenant with Him, He shares His perfection with you when the two of you become one. Therefore, your job is not to get yourself to heaven or make yourself perfect; your job is to come unto Christ, and He will get you to the Father. Then you have become perfect "in" and "through" Christ by the power of His Atonement.[18]

Stop worrying about whether or not you are going to make it and focus on the fact that you have obtained the principles and ordinances of the gospel necessary for you to go back to

Stop worrying and start acting

the Father's presence. Bruce R. McConkie gave a great hope for all of us striving to endure this mortal journey when he taught,

> If you're on that path and pressing forward, and you die, you'll never get off the path. There is no such thing as falling off the straight and narrow path in the life to come. . . . You don't have to live a life that's truer than true. You don't have to have an excessive zeal that becomes fanatical and becomes unbalancing. What you have to do is stay in the mainstream of the Church and live as upright and decent people live in the Church—keeping the commandments, paying your tithing, serving in the organizations of the Church, loving the Lord, staying on the straight and narrow path. If you're on that path when death comes—because this is the time and the day appointed, this the probationary estate—you'll never fall off from it, and, for all practical purposes, your calling and election is made sure.[19]

My counsel to you is to keep going and never give up. You have such a rich and exciting life ahead. So many great opportunities and possibilities to lift, build, love, and create Zion in your own home, ward, and community. If you falter along the way or are ashamed of post-mission choices you have made, "The joyful news for anyone who desires to be rid of the consequences of past poor choices is that the Lord sees weaknesses differently than He does rebellion. Whereas the Lord warns that unrepented rebellion will bring punishment, when the Lord speaks of weaknesses, it is always with mercy."[20] The Lord extends mercy along the pathway to perfection. Get His grace, get clean, and get on your way.

Elder M. Russell Ballard put his twist on enduring to the end: "Life isn't over for a Latter-day Saint until he or she is safely

How Will I Endure to the End through the Grace of Jesus Christ?

dead, with their testimony still burning brightly."[21] The path you travel in this life will be intertwined with many others seeking the kingdom of God. Allow the flame of your faith to help light the way not only for yourself, but for fellow travelers.

Personally, the most haunting verse in the scriptures comes from the vision Joseph Smith had of the three degrees of glory. After twenty verses describing the qualities of those who inherit the celestial kingdom, including two verses talking about those people "overcoming" all things with faith,[22] we encounter the qualities of those who inherit the terrestrial kingdom. "These are they who are not valiant in the testimony of Jesus" (D&C 76:79). This is the most noticeable difference between being sun or moon material. I call this verse haunting because each of us must evaluate whether or not we have chosen Christ and are actively following Him. Elijah once called out the people of Israel by asking, "How long halt ye between two opinions? If the Lord be God, follow him: but if Baal, then follow him." Sadly, "the people answered him not a word" (1 Kings 18:21). We cannot be fence sitters in the gospel. Discipleship demands decisive direction. Therefore, "decision determine destiny."[23] Choose Jesus Christ to guide whatever path you pursue, always keeping in mind the ultimate destination of your travels. Remember, "If you have not chosen the kingdom of God first, it will in the end make no difference what you have chosen instead."[24]

Take the Savior's counsel to "be of good cheer" (John 16:33). I believe that "the future is as bright as your faith."[25] I love you and wish you the best in all your celestial endeavors. I promise that you can make it home because "with God nothing shall be impossible" (Luke 1:37).

10 Questions to Answer
after Serving a Mission

Additional Readings

- Dieter F. Uchtdorf, "The Gift of Grace," *Ensign*, May 2015
- Dieter F. Uchtdorf, "Your Happily Ever After," *Ensign*, May 2010
- Dieter F. Uchtdorf, "Have We Not Reason to Rejoice," *Ensign*, November 2007
- David A. Bednar, "In the Strength of the Lord," *Ensign*, November 2004
- Bruce R. McConkie, "The Probationary Test of Mortality," Salt Lake Institute of Religion, January 10, 1982
- Stephen Robinson, *Believing Christ* and *Following Christ*
- Brad Wilcox, "His Grace Is Sufficient," BYU Devotional, July 12, 2011
- Sheri Dew, "Sweet Above All That Is Sweet," BYU Women's Conference, May 1, 2014

Notes

1. L. Tom Perry, "The Returned Missionary," *Ensign*, May 2001.
2. See D&C 1:30; 21:2; 64:33; 124:118; 136:38.
3. See David A. Bednar "In the Strength of the Lord," *Ensign*, November 2004.
4. Namely, Brad Wilcox, Sheri Dew, and Stephen Robinson.
5. Dieter F. Uchtdorf, "The Gift of Grace," *Ensign*, May 2015.
6. See D&C 19:18.
7. See Bruce R. McConkie, "The Purifying Power of Gethsemane," *Ensign*, May 1985.
8. See Luke 22:48.

How Will I Endure to the End through the Grace of Jesus Christ?

9. See John 18:13–29; Luke 23:3–11.

10. See Luke 22:63–65; Matthew 26:27.

11. See John 19:1.

12. Lee Strobel, *The Case for Christ*, (Edinburgh, Scotland: Thomas Nelson, 2013), 195.

13. Bruce R. McConkie, "The Purifying Power of Gethsemane."

14. Dietrich Bonhoeffer, *The Cost of Discipleship* (New York: Touchstone, 1995), 88.

15. Neal A. Maxwell, "Remember How Merciful the Lord Hath Been," *Ensign*, May 2004.

16. Thanks to Brother Robert Millet for sharing this beautiful truth with me.

17. Dieter F. Uchtdorf, "Have We Not Reason to Rejoice," *Ensign*, November 2007.

18. See Moroni 10:32–33 and D&C 76:69.

19. Bruce R. McConkie, "The Probationary Test of Mortality," Salt Lake Institute of Religion, January 10, 1982.

20. Richard G. Scott, "Personal Strength Through the Atonement of Jesus Christ," *Ensign*, November 2013.

21. M. Russell Ballard, as quoted by F. Burton Howard, "Commitment," *Ensign*, May 1996.

22. D&C 76:53, 60.

23. Thomas S. Monson, "Decisions Determine Destiny," BYU Devotional, November 6, 2005.

24. William Law, as quoted by Neal A. Maxwell, "Response to a Call," *Ensign*, May 1974.

25. Thomas S. Monson, "Be of Good Cheer," *Ensign*, May 2009.

About the Author

BENJAMIN HYRUM WHITE has a love for missionary work. He served as a full-time missionary in the Colorado Denver North Mission and worked at the MTC while in college. Ben wrote "The History of *Preach My Gospel*" for his master's degree at BYU. His other writings include *10 Questions to Answer While Preparing for a Mission* and the children's book *I Hope They Call Me on a Mission*. Brother White is a seminary teacher, and his biggest conversion was getting his beautiful wife, Keenan, to marry him! The Whites have five children, live in Utah Valley, and try to share the gospel in word and in deed.

0 26575 16607 1